AMERICANS
THE *Spirit* OF A *Nation*

HARRIET TUBMAN

"On My Underground Railroad I Never Ran My Train Off the Track"

R. Conrad Stein

E **Enslow Publishers, Inc.**
40 Industrial Road
Box 398
Berkeley Heights, NJ 07922
USA

http://www.enslow.com

"On my Underground Railroad I never ran my train off the track and I never lost a passenger."

Library of Congress Cataloging-in-Publication Data

Stein, R. Conrad.
    Harriet Tubman : "on my underground railroad I never ran my train off the track" /
    R. Conrad Stein.
    p. cm. — (Americans-the spirit of a nation)
    Includes bibliographical references and index.
    Summary: "Explores the life of Harriet Tubman, including her childhood in slavery and her escape, her Underground Railroad missions, her spy work during the Civil War, and her legacy in American history"—Provided by publisher.
    ISBN 978-0-7660-3481-5
    1. Tubman, Harriet, 1820?–1913—Juvenile literature. 2. Slaves—United States—Biography—Juvenile literature. 3. African American women—Biography—Juvenile literature. 4. African Americans—Biography—Juvenile literature. 5. Underground Railroad—Juvenile literature. I. Title.
    E444.T82S75 2010
    973.7'115092—dc22
    [B]
    2009012123

Printed in the United States of America

092009 Lake Book Manufacturing, Inc., Melrose Park, IL

10 9 8 7 6 5 4 3 2 1

To Our Readers:
We have done our best to make sure all Internet Addresses in this book were active and appropriate when we went to press. However, the author and the publisher have no control over and assume no liability for the material available on those Internet sites or on other Web sites they may link to. Any comments or suggestions can be sent by e-mail to comments@enslow.com or to the address on the back cover.

♻ Enslow Publishers, Inc., is committed to printing our books on recycled paper. The paper in every book contains 10% to 30% post-consumer waste (PCW). The cover board on the outside of each book contains 100% PCW. Our goal is to do our part to help young people and the environment too!

Illustration Credits: Associated Press, p. 112; Cayuga County Office of Tourism / explore nyarts.com, p. 107; Enslow Publishers, Inc., p. 49; The Granger Collection, New York, pp. 17, 33, 37, 43, 54, 58, 75, 79; Courtesy of Jay Meredith, Bucktown Village Museum, Bucktown, Maryland, pp. 9, 25; Jerry Schad / Photo Researchers, Inc., p. 29; Library of Congress, pp. 3, 6, 11, 20, 27, 38, 40, 48, 52, 55, 74, 77, 82, 84, 91, 93, 95, 98, 105, 109; Military and Historical Image Bank, p. 101; National Geographic / Getty Images, p. 72; © North Wind Picture Archives, pp. 14, 66, 103; Courtesy of Rensselaer County Historical Society, p. 89; Schomburg Center / Art Resource, NY, p. 63.

Cover Illustration: Library of Congress (Portrait of Harriet Tubman).

CONTENTS

Harriet Tubman

An Incident in the Life of a Slave Girl

When Harriet Tubman was twelve years old, she visited a store near her farm in rural Maryland. Suddenly, a white man burst into the store looking for a slave boy who had just run away from him. The boy saw the angry man approach and bolted outside. The man picked up a two-pound iron weight from the counter and threw it at the runaway. Harriet moved toward the door to protect the boy. The weight hit her on the forehead. She later said that the iron object "broke my skull and cut a piece of [my] shawl clean off and drove it into my head."[1]

Harriet was knocked unconscious. She had to be carried home, dazed and bleeding from the head.

In the months to come, Harriet Tubman recovered. However, the blow to her head left deep, unseen scars. Forever afterward she was afflicted with what people at the time called "sleeping sickness." Without warning, she would fall off into a deep sleep. These trance-like sleeping spells could occur in the middle of the day and while she was on her feet.

Scholars today believe Tubman suffered from temporal lobe epilepsy (TLE). This condition is often induced by a head injury. People with TLE commonly doze off for five- to fifteen-minute spells. They also tend to have vivid dreams and see strange visions during waking hours. Harriet had such visions and they brought her closer to God. She began believing she was watched, constantly, by a powerful spirit. The spirit protected her and served as her companion. It led her home when she was lost. Sometimes the spirit even allowed her to fly: "[I] used to dream of flying over fields and towns, and rivers and mountains, [and] looking down upon them."[2]

Harriet Tubman was born a slave. Perhaps her dreams of flying represented her hunger to be free.

2

> **THREE HUNDRED DOLLARS REWARD.**
>
> R ANAWAY from the subscriber on Monday the 17th ult., three negroes, named as follows: HARRY, aged about 19 years, has on one side of his neck a wen, just under the ear, he is of a dark chestnut color, about 5 feet 8 or 9 inches hight; BEN, aged aged about 25 years, is very quick to speak when spoken to, he is of a chestnut color, about six feet high; MINTY, aged about 27 years, is of a chestnut color, fine looking, and about 5 feet high. One hundred dollars reward will be given for each of the above named negroes, if taken out of the State, and $50 each if taken in the State. They must be lodged in Baltimore, Easton or Cambridge Jail, in Maryland.
>
> ELIZA ANN BRODESS,
> Near Bucktown, Dorchester county, Md.
> Oct. 3d, 1849.
>
> Delaware Gazette please copy

Enduring Slavery

A slave had no hope. One was born a slave, grew old, and died still in slavery. Throughout life a slave was subject to his or her owner's will and punishments. "No day ever dawns for the slave, nor is it looked for," said one freed black man reflecting on his past. "For the slave it is night—all night, forever."[1]

Young Minty

Harriet Tubman was probably born in 1820 or in 1822—no one knows for certain. She did not know the exact date of her birth. Few records were kept regarding the birthdates of slaves. No birthday parties were given for their children. Her childhood was devoted to work and little play. She never saw the inside of a schoolroom or learned to read or write. She once said, "I grew up like a neglected weed—ignorant of liberty, having no experience of it."[2]

As a child, her name was Araminta Ross. Family members called her Minty. She was the fifth of nine children, all of them slaves. Araminta was born and grew up in Dorchester County, Maryland.

> **"I grew up like a neglected weed— ignorant of liberty, having no experience of it."**

When Araminta was about five, a white woman, known only as Miss Susan, drove up to her farm in a buggy. She told Araminta's owners she needed a young girl to look after her baby. That day Araminta was "hired out." She was sent away with Miss Susan without even being allowed to say good-bye to her mother and father. Miss Susan gave the owners a small sum of money for the "use" of their slave. Little Minty received not a penny.

At Miss Susan's house, Araminta was given the baby. Araminta was so small she had to sit on the floor in order to hold the baby properly. At night she was ordered to

Thomas Jefferson

Slavery in the Land of the Free

"All men are created equal" read the bold words of the Declaration of Independence. Yet at the time Thomas Jefferson wrote the Declaration, slavery was practiced throughout the land. Jefferson, the country's third president, was himself a slaveowner. Slavery began in what would become the United States in 1619 when a ship brought twenty captive Africans to the small settlement of Jamestown, Virginia. In the early 1800s, slavery started to disappear in the northern states where small farms and light industry prevailed. The institution of slavery remained strong in the South. By 1860, roughly one-third of the people in the southern portion of the country were enslaved men, women, and children.[3] Despite the presence of slaves, Americans of the time boasted that they lived in the freest country on earth. The existence of slavery in what was hailed as the land of the free was a form of hypocrisy that is difficult to understand today.

rock the baby's cradle. If the baby cried, Araminta was beaten. Miss Susan kept a small whip near the cradle. She often beat Araminta several times in the course of a day. Once Araminta, fearing a whipping, ran away from Miss Susan and hid in a pigpen. She stayed hidden for so long she became hungry and had to fight the pigs for their feed of potato peelings and carrot heads.

Araminta worked for Miss Susan for many dismal months. All the time she remained homesick and fearful of punishment. Years later she recalled, "I used to sleep on the floor [in Miss Susan's house] and there I'd lie and cry and cry."[4]

Araminta was sick often as a young child. She caught fevers that were so high they seemed to be on the verge of burning her up. When she was home and not hired out, her mother nursed her through the long spells of illness. Often her mother sat by her bed and told her Bible stories. Her mother could not read, but she heard and memorized the stories from Sunday church services. Araminta listened, enraptured by the words of the Bible.

Araminta was an unusually quiet child. It was believed she was not bright enough to learn household chores. At home or when she was hired out, Araminta was sent to the fields to do farm work alongside the men. Often she cleared forestland. This involved cutting down trees and hauling away logs with a team of horses. She also became an expert at packing and hauling grain. Araminta became as efficient at this work as any man. Toiling in the woods allowed her to be alone with nature and with God. The forest became her friend and her sanctuary. In the future, her love and knowledge of the woods aided scores of people in their quest for freedom.

Minty's Life in Slavery

Araminta and her mother belonged to a man named Edward Brodess. Her mother, Rit, had already been passed on to various members of the Brodess family as if she were a bed or a chest of drawers. Rit worked as a cook in the Brodess home. Araminta's father, Ben Ross, was a skilled woodsman. He was owned by Dr. Anthony Thompson, who had a nearby plantation. Slave marriages had no legal basis. An owner could break up the marriage by selling the husband or the wife to some distant farm. Such a forced breakup did not happen to Araminta's parents. In fact, Dr. Thompson granted Ben his freedom when he turned forty-five years of age.

Occasionally, owners gave slaves freedom, especially when they grew old and their sale price declined. Ben Ross continued to work for the doctor as a free man. Working for Dr. Thompson allowed Ben to keep his marriage together. However, Ben's wife and children remained enslaved and subject to the whims of their owner.

Stories handed down from older family members claimed that Rit's mother, Araminta's grandmother, Modesty, was born in Africa. Her grandmother was said to come from the Ashanti people who lived in present-day Ghana. The Ashanti were known for the strength of their men and the independence of their women. Tribal members were also very respected for their wisdom.

From Africa, the Ashanti brought folk sayings and words to the wise, such as, "Don't test the depth of a river with both feet."[5]

Slaveholders discouraged blacks from talking about their African tribal identities. The owners feared that group loyalties based on African ethnic roots might make slaves more likely to revolt. Still, the slaves discussed African traditions and culture in secret. Whites also were aware of African ethnic groups. The whites valued Ashanti people for their strength. But whites said Ashantis made poor slaves because they were independent minded and rebellious by nature.

It is believed that Minty's grandmother came from the Ashanti people, who lived in present-day Ghana. A crowd of people watch two Ashanti men play a game in this illustration.

Anansi, Friend and Trickster

Generations of Ashanti parents told their children folk stories, some of which have survived to this day. A popular hero in one of the stories is Anansi, who is often portrayed as a spider. He is a mischievous spider who protects the Ashanti by tricking those who wish to harm them. In a popular story, the spider encounters a swarm of hornets that are about to sting the people of a village. Anansi tricks the hornets into thinking that it is raining and for their own safety they should return to their hives.

Slaves turned to religion to cope with their bitter circumstances. Owners usually granted their slaves a day of rest on Sunday. Owners encouraged their slaves to attend religious services. Sometimes a black preacher presided over the meetings. But the fear of massive slave revolutions began to haunt whites. Many whites believed black ministers were passing along messages of insurrection within their sermons. At the insistence of the owners, white preachers were called upon to give Sunday services to the enslaved. Often, after the white-approved church services, the slaves gathered in secluded spots and held their own church meetings. In the secret services, black preachers told their congregations the story of Moses who led his people out of slavery.

In many southern regions, slaves outnumbered whites. Whites in those areas lived in fear of slave uprisings. When Araminta was eleven years old, such a revolution broke out in nearby Virginia. A slave named Nat Turner (1800–1831) led the upheaval. A highly intelligent man, Turner learned to read on his own. He frequently disappeared in the fields and read the Bible. He came to believe God had given him a mission to free the slaves in the United States.

In August 1831, Turner and a band of followers broke away from their plantation and marched from farm to farm in rural Virginia. As they marched, they freed slaves and killed white people. Before he was captured, fifty-nine whites had died at Turner's hands.[6] Nat Turner was convicted of murder and was hanged on November 11, 1831. His was not the first or the only slave revolt that jolted the country. But the Nat Turner uprising was particularly violent and struck terror in the hearts of white people.

Young Araminta knew the Bible well. Friends said she could recite long biblical passages word for word. While working in the fields and forests, she prayed out loud. Sometimes her prayers took the form of a conversation with an unseen supreme being. She even prayed for her owner, Edward Brodess, who was cruel to his slaves: "Oh, Lord, convert ole master," she said in one

The capture of Nat Turner on October 30, 1831. He would later be executed. The revolt he led caused great fear among whites living in the South.

of her prayers, ". . . change [that] man's heart, and make him a Christian."[7]

A Changing World for Slaves

A master could beat his slaves, withhold food from them, or sell them to someone far away. Most slaves viewed being sold as their worst fate. Being sold meant leaving loved ones and being forced to live with strangers. But slaves were "property." Therefore, they were priced and sold on the market just as were horses or cows.

In the early 1800s, two developments profoundly changed the lives of American slaves. First, by law, the direct importation of slaves from Africa ended in 1808. This meant no new slaves could be taken from Africa or the Caribbean islands and sold to American buyers. The law was often violated, but it greatly slowed down the flow of slaves brought into the United States. Second, cotton became a major industry in the southern states. The cotton industry was boosted in 1793 when a young Massachusetts inventor, Eli Whitney, built the first cotton gin. Whitney's device was a simple, hand-cranked machine. It separated seeds from raw cotton fiber much faster than the old method, which was to separate the seeds from the cotton fiber by hand.

The expanding cotton industry and the law banning the importation of slaves from other countries greatly increased the price of slaves in the United States. Picking cotton was a laborious task, which required the work of many field hands. The demand for slaves became greater than the supply. Prices for strong field hands soared.

Farms in Georgia, Alabama, South Carolina, Mississippi, and Louisiana had the greatest need for additional slaves. These Deep South states were the country's major cotton producers. They employed small armies of field workers to harvest cotton and sugarcane. Slave owners in border states such as Virginia and Maryland studied the prices offered by the Deep South buyers. Many slaveholders in the border states had owned members of the same enslaved families for generations. Now, acting largely out of greed, the owners began selling their slaves.

Border state slaves learned of developments in the Deep South through whispered word and hearsay. Rumors of an impending sale terrified enslaved men and women in the border regions. All knew something was in the air, something that would break up their families. What little comfort and security a slave found in life came from family love.

Slaves at Araminta's farm feared the "Georgia traders." White men called Georgia traders commonly marched large groups of slaves from Maryland to the Deep South. The traders stopped at farms along the way, buying two or three slaves from each place before continuing their trek. The marching slaves were chained together. Many were in tears knowing they would never again see their families

When Araminta was in her late teens, she had grown to her full height of five feet.[8] Although frail and slight-looking, she was a tireless worker. Her owner, Edward

An idealized view of a cotton plantation in the Deep South state of Mississippi. The cotton industry greatly expanded in the South and required more slaves. Slaves in the border states, like Maryland, feared being sold to a Deep South plantation.

Brodess, had shown her to interested buyers. He presented her at work, hauling logs and driving horse-drawn carts. Brodess bragged that Araminta could outwork any male field hand he owned. Some owners in Maryland and Virginia were reluctant to sell their slaves because they knew the deep pain such a sale brought. Brodess had no such misgivings. He was in the process of buying more land and needed cash. Slaves represented ready funds.

As a young girl, Araminta had seen two of her older sisters sold. She reported they were, "taken away as part of a chain gang." She remembered the "agonized expression" on their faces and their "weeping and lamenting" as they were marched south.[9] Watching the girls being forced to leave their home was a family scar that never healed.

One day Araminta's mother, Rit, learned that Edward Brodess planned to sell her son to a Georgia man. She determined she would die rather than see her youngest son, Moses, taken away. She hid Moses in the woods for several weeks and later concealed him in her cabin. When Brodess pounded on the cabin door demanding the boy, Rit took up an ax. She declared, "The first man that comes into my house, I will split his head open."[10] Slaves sometimes won violent confrontations with a master. In this case, Brodess decided against facing a furious mother armed with an ax. He left the boy alone and peace prevailed. Rit's act of courage became a family legend.

> **"The first man that comes into my house, I will split his head open."**
>
> —Minty's mother, Rit

Marriage

In 1844, Araminta married John Tubman. Little is known about how the two met. John was a free black man who lived near Araminta's father, Ben Ross. A union between a free man and a slave woman presented many disadvantages. The law did not recognize such a marriage. The enslaved woman remained under the control of her owner despite her being married. Worse yet, slavery status followed the woman. By law, any baby born to an enslaved woman was a slave. It did not matter that the father was free. The Tubman couple never had children.

After her marriage, Araminta changed her first name to Harriet—the proper name of her mother, whom most people called Rit. She also took the last name of her

The Free African-American Community

Free blacks were numerous in the border states. In 1860, almost half the black population of Maryland was composed of free men and women.[11] There were far fewer free blacks in the Deep South. A slave could obtain freedom through various means. As a reward for faithful service, some owners freed their slaves. Some slaves purchased their freedom with the help of free family members. Still, others carefully saved the money they earned doing side jobs and bought their freedom. Saving one's money to buy freedom became far more difficult in the mid-nineteenth century when the price of slaves increased sharply.

husband: The young woman became Harriet Tubman. With that name she entered the history books.

Flight

In 1849, Harriet's owner, Edward Brodess, died suddenly at the age of forty-seven. His death threw the Brodess slaves into a state of panic. They believed they would almost immediately be sold. Enslaved people had seen this pattern before on neighboring farms. When the master died, the court awarded his slaves to various heirs, and they promptly sold them to the highest bidder. Brothers and sisters were scattered about to different areas of the South. Families were broken up, never to reunite again.

Scholars believe Harriet Tubman contemplated escape long before 1849 and the death of her master. Her religious beliefs had evolved to tell her the entire system of slavery was a sin. She wanted to be free and had grown tired of the abuses of slavery. But the act of breaking away held heavy consequences. If caught, she would be dragged back. Once home, she could be tied to a post and whipped for her attempt to escape. If successful she would leave a husband, her family, and the only home she ever knew.

Despite the dangers, Harriet Tubman was determined to escape and decide her own fate. She reasoned that if she waited much longer she would be taken away in a chain gang. Geography ruled her circumstances. In Maryland, she faced a hike of several days to reach the free states to the north. If she were sold to a Georgia

Sales of Human Beings

Being offered at a public sale was a humiliating and degrading experience for a slave. Enslaved people were lined up in ranks, sometimes naked, while prospective buyers examined them. Levi Coffin, a well-known Underground Railroad stationmaster, witnessed a slave sale and reported:

The men who intended to purchase [the slaves] passed from one to another of the group, examining them just as I would examine a horse I wished to buy. These men seemed devoid of any feeling of humanity, and treated the negroes as if they were brutes. They examined their limbs and teeth to see if they were sound and healthy. . . . It was disgusting to witness their actions, and to hear their vulgar and profane language. Now and then one of [the buyers] would make some obscene remark, and the rest would greet it with peals of laughter, but not a smile passed over the sad countenances of the slaves.[12]

THREE HUNDRED DOLLARS REWARD.

RANAWAY from the subscriber on Monday the 17th ult., three negroes, named as follows: HARRY, aged about 19 years, has on one side of his neck a wen, just under the ear, he is of a dark chestnut color, about 5 feet 8 or 9 inches hight; BEN, aged aged about 25 years, is very quick to speak when spoken to, he is of a chestnut color, about six feet high; MINTY, aged about 27 years, is of a chestnut color, fine looking, and about 5 feet high. One hundred dollars reward will be given for each of the above named negroes, if taken out of the State, and $50 each if taken in the State. They must be lodged in Baltimore, Easton or Cambridge Jail, in Maryland.

ELIZA ANN BRODESS,
Near Bucktown, Dorchester county, Md.
Oct. 3d, 1849.

☞The Delaware Gazette will please copy the above three weeks, and charge this office.

Eliza Brodess placed this reward notice in the Delaware Gazette *on October 3, 1849. A reward was placed on the heads of Harriet Tubman (Minty), and her brothers Ben and Harry (Henry) after they attempted to escape the Brodess farm.*

plantation, she would be many hundreds of miles from freedom. The time to act was now.

On a dark night in September of 1849, Tubman and two of her brothers set out on a road. The free lands they knew about were Pennsylvania and New Jersey, which lay to the north. But how far north would they have to walk to reach freedom? How could they be certain they were walking in a northerly direction? The three argued as they walked. Finally, the two brothers lost courage and decided to go back. Harriet followed them, deeply disappointed.

It is unclear how long Harriet and her brothers were gone or if they suffered punishment on their return. It is known that Eliza Brodess offered a reward for their capture. An advertisement appearing in the *Delaware Gazette* on October 3, 1849, described the two brothers. It said of the other escapee: "MINTY, aged about 27 years, is of a chestnut color, fine looking, and about 5 feet high. One hundred dollars reward will be given for each of the [three] above named negroes."[13] Though her first attempt at escaping had failed, the fire of freedom still burned within Harriet. She would have her freedom or die in the attempt to be free. Her biographer, Sarah Bradford, interviewed her years later and wrote Tubman's words: "I had reasoned [this] out in my mind; there was one of two things I had a right to, liberty, or death; if I could not have one, I would have [the other]; for no man should take me alive."[14]

The North Star

Abolitionist societies flourished in the northern United States during the 1850s. The societies were made up of men and women devoted to ending—*abolishing*—the practice of slavery. The various groups met, sang songs, listened to speakers, and signed petitions demanding their government put an immediate end to slavery. One of their favorite songs was "The Abolitionist's Hymn":

> *We mourn not that man should toil;*
> *'Tis nature's need, 'tis God's decree;*
> *But let the hand that tills the soil*
> *Be, like the wind that fans it, free.*[1]

Harriet Tubman accepted the help of abolitionist groups as she made her flight to freedom. She later joined the movement and became one of the country's leading abolitionists.

The North Star Leads to Freedom

The exact date of Tubman's second escape attempt is uncertain. It may have happened shortly after she returned following her failed attempt with her brothers. On a night in the fall of 1849, Tubman took to the road once more. This time she ventured out alone. She did not even tell her husband of her plans. Some authors have suggested she was afraid he would betray her.

She did leave a coded message with a slave girl named Mary. She hoped Mary would pass the message on to her mother. Tubman's farewell came in the form of a song. On the night she broke away, she stood outside Mary's window and sang a well-known hymn:

I'm sorry I'm going to leave you,
Farewell, oh farewell;
But I'll meet you in the morning,
Farewell, oh farewell.
I'll meet you in the morning,
I'm bound for the promised land,
On the other side of Jordan,
Bound for the promised land.[2]

Armed with courage and a hunger for freedom, she began a solitary flight. Perhaps, to bolster her courage, she sang a song in her heart.

Her plans were vague. She had determined that her destination was the state of Pennsylvania, which shared a border with Maryland. Pennsylvania was a free state, a place where slavery was forbidden. She learned about the North from secret conversations with other slaves. Enslaved men and women often fled from Maryland to northern free states. The 1850 Maryland census reported 259 slaves had run away from their masters in the state.[3] It is believed the number is much higher because many owners did not report all escapees.

Tubman decided to walk by night and hide in the woods during the day. Slaves were not allowed on the roads without written permission from their owner. Any white person could stop a black and demand to see his or her pass. At night, she would encounter few, if any people. Walking at night was scary, but it was safer than trying to move about during the day.

In the dark, lonely night, Harriet Tubman looked into the sky and found the Big Dipper. By tracing an imaginary line through the "handle" of the Big Dipper she saw the North Star. This is the one star that does not appear to move

The Big Dipper (top of photo) contains the North Star in its handle. Tubman looked to the sky to find the Big Dipper to guide her north.

The North Star, Path to Freedom

To the slaves, the North Star assumed an almost mystical importance. It was a God-given light shining on their path to freedom. Some compared it to the pillar of fire that guided Moses and his followers out of Egypt and to the Promised Land. Frederick Douglass, the famous escaped slave, published an abolitionist newspaper he called *The North Star*. Slaves called the Big Dipper the Drinking Gourd. A favorite song, whose words were a musical map to freedom, said:

> *Follow the drinking gourd,*
> *Follow the drinking gourd,*
> *For the old man is a-waiting*
> *For to carry you to freedom,*
> *Follow the drinking gourd.*[4]

in the sky. Walking toward the North Star was another strategy for escape she learned from other slaves.

A Passenger on a Secret Railroad

From the beginning, Harriet Tubman decided she would accept help under the right conditions. But taking assistance from others was a tricky business. She never forgot that on her last attempt Eliza Brodess offered a one-hundred-dollar reward for information leading to her capture. One hundred dollars in those days fed a large family for many months. Some men, the dreaded slave catchers, made their living by hunting down runaways and collecting rewards. Yet she determined she need not fear all strangers. Tubman believed there were religious people living in rural Maryland. A true Christian abolitionist would help her escape without any thought of a reward. The problem lay in deciding whom she could trust.

Tubman had encountered an abolitionist who helped her. Before she escaped, she talked to a white woman who lived near her owner's farm. She never disclosed the woman's name because she wanted to spare her having trouble with the law. Historians today believe the woman might have been Hannah Leverton, an antislavery Quaker who lived in Caroline County.[5] Quakers, Tubman would soon learn, were zealous in their work to end slavery in the United States. The woman gave Tubman a piece of paper with two names written on it. The paper meant little to Tubman because she could not read. The woman then described a house along the road to the north. She advised Tubman to knock on the door and present the paper to whoever answered.

Tubman reached the house during the night. She waited in the woods until dawn. Gathering all her courage, she knocked on the door. A woman answered and Tubman gave her the piece of paper. The woman handed her a broom and told her to sweep the porch. This was an odd request considering the two had just met. Still, Tubman started sweeping vigorously. She would later discover that deception was a key tactic used by people who helped slaves to break away. Neighbors would think Tubman was a servant doing household chores. They would not suspect she was a runaway slave. Tubman stored this lesson in her mind. Disguising one's true activity was a trick that she would use in the future when she led slaves out of bondage.

By knocking on the door of that Maryland farmhouse, Harriet Tubman made her first contact with the Underground Railroad. In the years to come, she would rise to fame working for this organization. Some writers would call Harriet Tubman the Queen of the Underground Railroad.

Historians today heap praise on the courageous men and women of the Underground Railroad. It was not a railroad, nor did it run underground. In fact, it was not even an organization in the true sense. The Underground Railroad was a secret network of Americans, black and white, who assisted slaves on their flights to freedom. Helping slaves escape violated the law. Anyone coming to the aid of a fugitive slave faced fines and a prison sentence. Because everyone involved was a lawbreaker, the Underground Railroad was a hush-hush and loosely organized group. Members knew only a few fellow members. The men and women agents used railroad terms to further disguise their activities. Escaped slaves were "passengers." Houses where an escapee could find assistance were "stations." Those who owned the houses were "stationmasters." People who escorted the slaves over roads were "conductors."

Runaway slaves depicted traveling along the Underground Railroad in 1838. Tubman made her first contact with the Underground Railroad when she escaped in 1849.

Harriet Tubman spent several hours with the female Underground Railroad agent. Later that evening, the woman's husband put Tubman in a horse-drawn wagon and covered her with canvas. Thus concealed, he drove her to another farmhouse farther north, which served as the next "station" on the Underground Railroad. In this way, station by station, Tubman approached the state of Pennsylvania.

Crossing the Line

The state of Pennsylvania lay roughly one hundred miles from Tubman's Maryland farm.[6] Her journey

The Underground Railroad Gets Its Name

Legend says the Underground Railroad got its name in 1831 when a slave named Tice Davids broke away. Davids' master pursued him to the town of Ripley, Ohio. Once in Ripley, Davids was hidden in a basement by an antislavery man named John Rankin. The owner walked the streets of Ripley completely baffled by his slave's disappearance. The puzzled owner was heard to say, "[He] must have gone off on an underground railroad."[7] Thus, according to lore, the name Underground Railroad was born.

probably took at least a week to complete. She accepted help from several households along the way. Often she traveled alone at night with only the stars as her companions.

Somewhere Harriet Tubman crossed the Mason-Dixon Line. This line was drawn up in the 1760s by the surveyors Charles Mason and Jeremiah Dixon. Originally it was surveyed to end property disputes between residents of Pennsylvania and their southern neighbors. Then, in the years before the Civil War, the Mason-Dixon Line took on a higher importance. The line served as the all-important boundary between slave states and free states.

On a rural road, Tubman met a passerby and asked where she was. She received the answer: Pennsylvania! This was her goal, the glorious land of freedom. She later said, "When I found I had crossed that line, I looked at my hands to see if I was the same person. There was such glory over everything; the sun came like gold through the trees and over the fields, and I felt like I was in heaven."[8]

"When I found I had crossed that line, I looked at my hands to see if I was the same person."

Late in 1849, Harriet Tubman arrived in Philadelphia. She soon learned the city offered mixed blessings to African Americans. Many blacks thrived in Philadelphia, but others lived in fear.

Freedom in Philadelphia

Around her, Tubman saw businesses and institutions run by African Americans. Black street vendors sold flowers, oysters, and corn roasted in its husks. A black-run library provided books. Blacks met and discussed issues at Philadelphia's Free African Society, founded in 1787. The Mother Bethel African Methodist Church stood at the corner of 6th and Lombard Streets and welcomed parishioners. Philadelphia's schools were segregated, but at least African-American children learned to read.

Still, racial problems gripped the city. In 1850, Philadelphia was the country's second largest city, after

New York. Almost 10 percent of its population of 122,000 were blacks.[9] Many of the city's whites were new immigrants from Europe. Immigrants competed with African Americans for jobs. Tension ruled the crowded streets. Minor arguments between white and black young men escalated into fistfights and even gun battles. Gangs of whites with names like the Blood Tubs and the Rats roamed the city's streets attacking blacks.

Adding to the city's strife were the slave catchers. They were a class of men considered to be so vile they were shunned even by whites who disliked their black neighbors. Slave catchers lived on rewards paid by owners. They captured runaway men and women, dragged them south, and sought payment from the master. Some slave catchers seized free Philadelphia blacks and sold them as slaves in the South. Forcibly taking a man or woman captive was kidnapping, a violation of Pennsylvania law. Slave catchers paid little attention to laws. They sought only money.

A House Dividing

For decades, Americans were locked in heated arguments over slavery. Often religion entered into the arguments. One side claimed God condemned slavery while the other said God approved of the institution. Both sides pointed to passages in the Bible to prove their points. The arguments were always left unresolved. Slavery remained legal in almost half of the country. In the South, it was politely called "our peculiar institution."

Tubman arrived in Philadelphia in late 1849. This is a view of Chestnut Street in Philadelphia from the 1860s.

The extension of slavery into the states opening to the west started a new chapter in the bitter debate. The abolitionists demanded the West be made up of free states. Proslavery men and women believed the institution of slavery should follow the country's western expansion. Trying to soothe tempers, Congress passed an act called the Compromise of 1850. The act forbade slavery in the new state of California, but it allowed the institution in New Mexico and Utah if the settlers there approved.

As a part of the Compromise of 1850, Congress enacted the Fugitive Slave Law. Laws regarding the treatment of runaway slaves dated back to the 1790s.

The Fugitive Slave Law of 1850 outraged abolitionists. This anti-Fugitive Slave Law cartoon was published in 1850. This law made Tubman's life much more insecure.

The 1850 Fugitive Slave Law called for increased penalties, including long prison terms to anyone assisting a runaway slave. Many people at that time believed the law was aimed

"I was free, and *they* should be free."

directly at the Underground Railroad. The new law also required police and sheriffs to arrest escapees even in free states such as Pennsylvania. The Fugitive Slave Law of 1850 was cursed and condemned by abolitionists. It legitimatized the activities of the hated slave catchers. In theory at least, local police would have to cooperate with the men who made their living rounding up fugitives.

Harriet Tubman was aware of the furor caused by the Fugitive Slave Law of 1850. She was an escapee. Certainly the law made her life even more insecure. If captured, she would be returned to a life of slavery. Nevertheless she continued to live in a black neighborhood in Philadelphia. In order to survive, she worked in kitchens for low pay.

Despite what must have been almost constant fear, Tubman dedicated her life to a new goal. Her brothers, sisters, nieces, and nephews were still held as slaves in Maryland. Tubman determined she would take the ultimate risk and return to the land of slavery to rescue her family. She said, simply, "I was free, and *they* should be free."[10]

4

Riding the Underground Railroad to Glory

Harriet Tubman began her rescue missions to bring her family members north to freedom. Her work expanded when she became associated with the Underground Railroad. Eventually, she rose to become the most famous of all conductors on that secret railway to freedom. Her work on the Underground Railroad drew praise from all those Americans who hated slavery. Fellow escaped slave and abolitionist Frederick Douglass said of her,

"The midnight sky and the silent stars have been the witnesses of your devotion to freedom and of your heroism. . . . I know of no one who has willingly encountered more perils and hardships to serve our enslaved people than you have."[1]

First Mission

Shortly after the passage of the 1850 Fugitive Slave Law, word reached Tubman of troubles in her old Maryland home. She learned that her favorite niece, Kessiah, was to be sold. It is unknown exactly how Tubman received this distressing news. Perhaps it came to her from an escaped slave who was a friend of the family. After hearing this news, Tubman reasoned she had no choice but to act swiftly. She must go back to Maryland and rescue her niece.

Very few escapees returned to the South. The risks were simply too great. But Harriet Tubman began to believe it was her duty—her mission ordered by God—to lead slaves to freedom. Was she afraid to journey back to the South? Most certainly she was afraid and her fears came out in her conversations with God. She once said, "The Lord told me to do this [go to the South and liberate slaves]. I said, 'Oh Lord, I can't—don't ask me—take someone else.'" Then the Lord told her, in a commanding voice, "It's you I want, Harriet Tubman."[2] Despite her fears, Tubman obeyed the word of God.

Tubman had an elaborate plan to rescue her niece. Details of that plan had to be passed on to everyone involved. The precise method of communication she used is unknown. Perhaps her early contacts with the Underground Railroad allowed her to spread the word of her arrival in Maryland. Somehow, a complicated string of messages and instructions was passed along from one nameless person to another. Through this secret message network, Tubman learned Kessiah was to be sold at auction in Cambridge, Maryland. Also offered for sale were Kessiah's two young children. One of her children was six years old; the other a baby. Potential buyers were not required to purchase the children if they were interested only in the mother.

Days before the scheduled sale, Tubman entered Baltimore, Maryland. She never said how she got to the city or how long the journey took. Baltimore lay on the west side of the Chesapeake Bay. This was land she had never seen before. Slave catchers freely prowled the roads in Maryland. In Baltimore, she hid in the house of friends. She received assistance from her brother-in-law, Tom Tubman, other Dorchester County free blacks, and slaves who lived and worked on Baltimore's busy waterfront.

Secretly, Tubman made contact with John Bowley, Kessiah's husband. Bowley was a free black man who worked as a shipbuilder. Many African Americans, both free men and slaves, were drawn to the sea. Ships carried people away from the United States where slavery was practiced. Black abolitionist Frederick Douglass was a caulker and ship's carpenter. Douglass once called ships "freedom's swift-winged angels, that fly round the world."[3]

This is a view of Baltimore harbor in 1836. Tubman stayed in Baltimore during her first rescue mission when she helped her niece, Kessiah, and her family escape from a slave auction.

Rescuing Kessiah

The city of Cambridge, Maryland, where the slave auction was to be held, was the capital of Dorchester County. Cambridge was on the east side of Chesapeake Bay. Thus, a large body of water separated Tubman from her niece. The public auction was held outside of the courthouse in the center of town. Kessiah stood on the courthouse steps with her two children. The bidding began. One wonders what thoughts raced through Kessiah's mind. At that moment, she was not a human being. She was a thing, no more important than a farm implement. She could be bought and taken away as property. Perhaps she would be sold to a Deep South buyer. Perhaps she would never see her children again. Such thoughts no doubt instilled terror within her. But Kessiah knew a rescue plan was in place. With all her heart, she hoped the plan would soon unfold.

The high bidder for Kessiah was a black man. This bidder was John Bowley, Kessiah's husband. On very few occasions, relatives saved enough money to buy freedom for their kin. The auctioneer was satisfied with Bowley's bid. Confident the sale was concluded, the auctioneer went to lunch. When he returned, he discovered Kessiah, her husband, and the children were gone. All had disappeared.

The purchase of Kessiah and her children was a ruse. It was part of a plan probably dreamed up with the help of Harriet Tubman. Bowley pretended he had enough money in his pocket to buy his wife and her children. In fact, he did not have nearly enough money for the purchase. But by claiming he had the funds, Kessiah and her children were taken to the side of the courthouse where the details of the sale were to be worked out. While arranging these details, the family managed to steal away and hide in a nearby house.

That night, Bowley took his wife and children to the Cambridge waterfront. All were wanted by the law, and they had to sneak through the streets. Bowley put his family on board a small boat, which might have been nothing more than a log canoe. He then sailed across Chesapeake Bay to Baltimore. Crossing the Chesapeake was dangerous, especially in a rickety boat. The waters were rough and a fierce wind screamed over the waves.

But Bowley was an experienced seaman. He made the trip and joined Tubman on the Baltimore shore.

From Baltimore, Harriet Tubman took the newly liberated family to Philadelphia. She later said little about the return overland trip. All that is known today is that the mission was successful. Harriet Tubman had liberated her first slaves.

The fact that the family turned to Tubman to execute the escape stands as a testament to their trust in her courage and her intelligence. It was only a year since her liberation. Family members believed that if anyone could save Kessiah and her children, it was Harriet Tubman.

A Family Free and United

Tubman felt her work was incomplete. She still had brothers and sisters held in bondage. She learned that her brother Moses was hired out to a farm north of Dorchester County. Once more, she risked her freedom to return to Maryland. She made this journey about a year after rescuing her niece. She met with her brother who was accompanied by two enslaved friends who were also eager to escape.

Tubman led all three men north to freedom. The group traveled mostly at night. When possible, Tubman followed the North Star. On cloudy nights, she used rivers as a guide. She knew most rivers in this part of Maryland flowed north to south. By walking alongside of the river, in an upstream direction, she headed steadily north.

Harriet Tubman took her brother and his two companions all the way to Philadelphia. The group arrived in the city in the late spring of 1851. Just months later, she returned to Maryland. This time she journeyed to her old home in Dorchester County. Her return was the most dangerous trip she had yet attempted. People in Dorchester County knew she was a fugitive. As a slave, she had been hired out to nearby farms and her face was familiar. Still, she made the trip because, she reasoned, God had ordered her to do so.

On a dark night late in 1851, she stood a short distance away from her husband's cabin. Through another person, she sent word asking her husband to come out and meet her. Her husband, John Tubman, was a free man and could more or less go where he pleased. But he refused even to go outside and talk to his wife. Harriet Tubman later learned John had remarried.

Tubman had not seen her husband for two years. His refusal to talk with her upset her deeply. One of her biographers reported that, at first, "[she] thought she would go right in [to John's cabin] and make all the trouble she could."[4] Later, she calmed down. She said that "he [John Tubman] dropped out of [my] heart."[5]

This 1851 journey proved to be a major operation. Tubman had gone to Maryland hoping to liberate more of her brothers and sisters. But her reputation proceeded her. Other slaves, hungry for freedom, had heard that she was on her way to Maryland. When Tubman encountered her brother, William Henry, she discovered he had acquired friends. Perhaps as many as eleven slaves, including her brother, waited to be rescued by the new Moses.[6] Tubman led the entire group north.

Safety in Canada

To Tubman, the Mason-Dixon Line was no longer the gateway to freedom for escapees. The Fugitive Slave Law had made every state, including Pennsylvania, a dangerous place to take refuge. Tubman decided to take her group out of the country. As she later said, "I wouldn't trust Uncle Sam with my people no longer, but I brought 'em clear off to Canada."[7]

While passing through New York State on the way to Canada, Tubman and her party stayed briefly with fellow escaped slave Frederick Douglass. The Douglass house in Rochester, New York, was a station on the Underground Railroad. To protect each other, Douglass and Tubman never acknowledged they met. But Douglass was no doubt referring to the Tubman-led group when he wrote: "On one occasion I had eleven fugitives at the same time under my roof, and it was necessary for them to remain with me until I could collect sufficient money to get them on to Canada. It was the largest number I ever had at any one time."[8]

> "I wouldn't trust Uncle Sam with my people no longer, but I brought 'em clear off to Canada."

From Rochester, the fugitives journeyed north to Canada. Tubman brought her followers across the border to St. Catharines, Canada, in December 1851.

Frederick Douglass

Frederick Douglass

Frederick Douglass (1818–1895) was born a slave in Talbot County, Maryland. When he was a child, the wife of one of his owners broke the law and taught him how to read a few words from a book. Most states had laws against teaching reading and writing to slaves because such knowledge increased their desires for freedom. Douglass mastered reading largely on his own. Sometimes he met with poor white children and gave them bread in return for books and help reading.

At age twenty, Douglass escaped and journeyed to New Bedford, Massachusetts. There, he joined abolitionist groups and became a powerful public speaker. In 1845, he published his autobiography *Narrative of the Life of Frederick Douglass, an American Slave.* The book sold thousands of copies and made Frederick Douglass famous. In the years before the Civil War, Frederick Douglass was one of the nation's leading abolitionists.

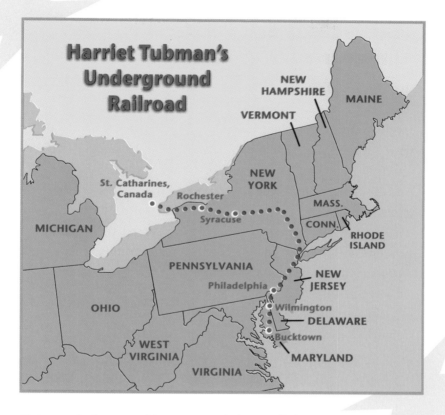

Tubman led some of her escaped slaves all the way to Canada. This is the escape route she would often use, which ended in St. Catharines, Canada.

The weather in their new country was freezing. The slaves had never experienced such bitter cold. They had no money. Many got jobs chopping timber in the woods. Chopping wood was painful work because the former slaves had no gloves and no proper winter coats. But, thanks to Harriet Tubman, they had freedom for the first time in their lives.

Harriet Tubman and the Underground Railroad

In 1849, a Talbot County, Maryland, newspaper called the *Easton Star* wrote: "RUNAWAYS. On Saturday night week, three slaves belonging to H. L. Edmondson, Esq., made their escape." The newspaper article then complained that "[a]lmost every week we hear of one or more slaves making their escape and if something is not speedily done to put a stop to it, that kind of property will hardly be worth owning. There seems to be some system about this business, and we strongly suspect they are assisted in their escape by an organized band of abolitionists."[9]

As this newspaper article points out, slaveholders regarded escaping slaves as theft of their "property." The newspaper correctly assumed that many of the escapees were aided by "an organized band of abolitionists." That band was the Underground Railroad, which was particularly active in the border state of Maryland.

Who were the men and women of the Underground Railroad? Importantly, many of them were women. This was at a time when women could not vote. In many states, unmarried females could not even own property such as homes and farms. Perhaps because they were denied basic rights, women felt a closer identity to slaves than men did.

Many African Americans served on the Underground Railroad, too. Free blacks took the greatest risks. If a free African American were caught aiding escapees, he or she faced a long prison term, usually longer than a white accused of the same "crime." A court could force a free black into slavery as punishment.

People of all religions were Underground Railroad workers, but the Quaker Church was most prominent. Quakers believed all humans were equal in the eyes of God. Therefore, to enslave a person because of the color of his or her skin was a crime committed against the Lord.

Harriet Tubman became associated with the Underground Railroad sometime around 1850, when she met many of the secret workers. Two workers—Thomas Garrett and William Still—had the greatest influence on her work as a "conductor."

Garrett, A Famous Stationmaster

Thomas Garrett (1789–1871) was a successful business-man who owned an iron manufacturing firm and a hardware store in Wilmington, Delaware. His house served as a station on the Underground Railroad. Slavery was fading in Delaware in the 1850s, but assisting escapees remained a severe violation of state law. Yet Garrett openly let it be known that runaways could find rest and food at his house. Garrett was a Quaker. True to Quaker beliefs, he considered lying to be a grave sin. If a judge or a police officer asked if he assisted escapees, he had no choice but to say yes.

In 1848, Garrett was brought to trial. He admitted in court that he helped fugitive slaves because it was impossible for him to tell a lie. He was fined fifteen

Thomas Garrett openly assisted runaway slaves. Garrett gave a lot of money to the abolitionist cause and he often helped Tubman when she stopped in Wilmington, Delaware.

hundred dollars by a judge.[10] In those days, that amount of money was enough to buy a farm. Despite the stiff fine, Garrett said he would continue to aid escapees. At his trial he announced to a crowded courtroom, " . . . if any of you know of any poor slave who needs assistance, send him to me. . . . [I will] never neglect an opportunity to assist a slave to obtain freedom."[11]

For Harriet Tubman, the Garrett house was one of the most important stations on her northward journey on the Underground Railroad. She arrived at the Garrett home regularly, unannounced and usually accompanied by several runaways. Always, Garrett assisted her and her band of fugitives. Garrett was wealthy. He often gave money to the cause of freedom. Many times Tubman used his donations to buy train tickets for herself and her followers.

Garrett recalled one of his surprise meetings with Tubman. She knocked on his door and said, "Mr. Garrett, I am here again, out of money, and with no shoes to my feet, and God has sent me to you for what I need."[12] Garrett claimed he was short of funds because he had just bought clothing for a large group of escapees.

Still, he gave money to Tubman because he so admired her courage and dedication to the abolitionist cause. He also was in awe of her spirituality, her sense of God-given purpose. He once said, "I never met with any person of any color who had more confidence in the voice of God, as spoken directly to her soul."[13]

Aside from assisting Tubman and other conductors, Garrett worked on his own to transport fugitives to the North. He used clever ploys to assist runaways. On several occasions, he gave escaped slaves rakes and hoes and marched them through Wilmington's streets. In this manner, he looked like a master supervising a work crew. When the fugitives were safely out of town, he collected the tools, sent the slaves on their way, and carried the tools back to his hardware store.

William Still, Father of the Railroad

William Still (1821?–1902) was born a free black in New Jersey. As a young man, he moved to Philadelphia where he joined abolitionist groups and supported the Underground Railroad. He ran a successful coal business in Philadelphia. Still also helped many escaped slaves settle in the city and other Pennsylvania communities. Eventually, he became known as the Father of the Underground Railroad.

Still was a prime organizer and administrator of the secret railroad operation. He did not venture into slave states to rescue people, as did Harriet Tubman. However, he was usually the first railroad worker to greet

William Still was usually the first person to greet escapees when they arrived in Philadelphia. He helped many escaped slaves settle in Pennsylvania.

escapees when they came to Philadelphia. Still worked for the Pennsylvania Anti-Slavery Society, an influential abolitionist group. In this capacity, he interviewed escaped slaves. While Still was born into freedom, some of his brothers and sisters were enslaved. When interviewing one newly escaped slave, Peter Friedman, Still was shocked to discover the man was his brother whom he had never seen before. In 1872, Still published a book called *The Underground Rail Road*. This book is a vital tool for scholars today who research this amazing chapter in American history.

Harriet Tubman and William Still were friends and coworkers in Philadelphia. Still admired her. He said in his book:

> *Her success was wonderful. Time and again she made successful visits to Maryland on the Underground Rail Road, and would be absent for weeks at a time, running daily risks while making preparations for herself and her passengers. Great fears were entertained for her safety, but she seemed wholly devoid of personal fear. The idea of being captured by slave-hunters or slave-holders, seemed never to enter her mind.*[14]

5

The Moses of Her People

T ubman's work to free family members served as a training ground for her future undertakings. After bringing her family to the North, she returned again and again to the southern state of Maryland and helped other slaves to escape. On each journey into slave country, she learned new methods as to how to lead people to freedom. She also strengthened her ties with Underground Railroad households, which lay on secret paths called "liberty lines."[1]

Comparisons With Moses

The first person to give Harriet Tubman the name of Moses was abolitionist William Lloyd Garrison in 1855. She would frequently be referred to as Moses in letters and newspapers from 1859 throughout the Civil War years. In 1869, Sarah Bradford published a book called *Scenes in the Life of Harriet Tubman.* Later she wrote a second edition of the book and titled it *Harriet Tubman, the Moses of Her People.* In the preface of the second book, published in 1886, Bradford said:

> *The title I have given my black heroine, in this second edition of her story, The Moses of Her People, may seem a little ambitious, considering that this Moses was a woman. . . . But I only give her here the name by which she was familiarly known, both at the North and the South, during the years of terror of the Fugitive Slave Law, and during our last Civil War.*[2]

It is unclear exactly how many times Tubman journeyed to the South and how many slaves she freed in the course of her work. Sarah Bradford said, "So she went nineteen times, and so she brought away over three hundred pieces of living and breathing 'property,' with God given souls."[3] Many modern scholars believe the Bradford numbers are exaggerated. One highly praised book on Tubman, published in 2004, says she made thirteen trips to the South and freed about seventy slaves.[4] Another author, writing in 2005, said she directly helped seventy people escape and gave instructions allowing fifty more to break for freedom.[5] All Tubman said about her work was that "On my Underground Railroad I never ran my train off the track and I never lost a passenger."[6]

Tubman returned to her home state, Maryland, when conducting her incursions into the South. The Underground Railroad operated three liberty lines from Maryland to Pennsylvania. The liberty line she used most often ran through Wilmington, Delaware, and the home of Thomas Garrett.

Tricks of the Trade

At various times, Harriet Tubman lived in Philadelphia, upstate New York, and in Canada. Always she held low-paying jobs, usually in kitchens. Carefully she saved the few pennies she earned to help pay for her missions to the South.

Sometimes an ex-slave would approach Tubman and ask her to liberate a son, a daughter, a wife, or some

Tubman biographer Sarah Bradford claimed Tubman helped three hundred slaves escape to freedom. Modern scholars believe this number is exaggerated. This is an engraving of Tubman made after the frontispiece to Bradford's 1869 book, Scenes in the Life of Harriet Tubman.

other relative. The person usually gave her some money to facilitate the mission. Tubman would start out with the intention of helping perhaps two or three specific people (usually family and close friends). But then the word was circulated in slave quarters: "Moses is coming, Moses is coming." When she got to her destination, she would find four or five others had joined the people who made up her original quest. All were hungry for freedom, and Tubman took everyone. One of her biographers claims she could escort as many ten freedom-seeking people on a northward journey.[7]

Some of the rescue efforts Tubman made in the 1850s are not well documented in terms of time and dates. It is not always known exactly when and where she performed some of her feats. But the amazing devices she used to take her bands to freedom are well documented. These tricks of the trade have added to the Tubman legend.

It is believed that beginning in 1852, Tubman made at least one and as many as two trips a year to the South.[8] There was a brief two-year period from 1858 to 1860 where it became too dangerous for her to go to Maryland. Beyond that, she would never be deterred from her mission.

Tubman preferred to travel in the winter months. Some of her journey was made at night and on foot. Winter travel was cruel, given the snow, cold, and freezing rain. She and her charges often had to hide in the woods and suffer through the harsh weather without shelter. But winter was the ideal time for her to do her Underground Railroad work. As a friend once wrote:

"She always came in the winter, when the nights are long and dark, and the people who have homes stay in them."[9]

The "Charm"

Harriet Tubman believed she possessed a mystical ability to sense trouble before it happened. If she felt slave catchers might be poised on the road ahead, she told her followers to hide under the trees. When her same mysterious "sense" said the road was clear, she led her people forward. Even she did not know the source of her ability to escape detection. She claimed she followed an inner voice. Tubman said that when she felt danger was near, her heart would, "go flutter, flutter."[10] Slaves called Tubman's amazing gift the "charm." William Wells Brown, a black author and a runaway slave, interviewed a fugitive who escaped with Tubman's help: "[The] whites can't catch Moses, 'cause you see she's born with the charm. The Lord has given Moses the power."[11]

> "[The] whites can't catch Moses, 'cause you see she's born with the charm."

Strangely, very little is written about how Harriet Tubman's uncontrollable sleeping spells affected her work. From time to time, her seizures or sleeping sickness hampered Tubman. Even when a slave catcher was in hot pursuit of her and her band, she could fall into a trance. Her followers knew ahead of time that she was subject to fade away into slumber. They simply waited out these periods of unexpected sleep. To some, the trance-like bouts added to her image of spirituality. The silent, sleeping times were periods when Moses talked to God. However, it must have been harrowing for her followers to stay calm and patient until their leader woke up.

Various sicknesses struck Tubman and her escapees while they were on the run. She dealt with the maladies the best way she could. On some occasions, she helped women carrying babies. Crying babies can expose people trying to hide. Tubman carried paregoric, a medicine that put the babies to sleep. She gave the babies the medicine only if she feared their crying would expose her party. During one escape effort, Tubman suffered from a violent toothache. She could not stop to get a doctor's medical help. So she knocked the painful tooth out of her mouth with a rock.[12]

Not one of the escapees Tubman supervised was ever captured. She achieved this incredible record of success because she was brave, determined, and very clever.

Deceiving the Slave Catchers

Often she returned to Dorchester County, Maryland, where many white slaveholders knew her face. But Tubman was a master at disguise. She managed to travel the roads near her old home without being recognized. Once she bought two live chickens at a market and carried the birds down the main street of a town. Thus, she played the role of a servant on an errand. Ahead, she saw a white man she knew. She pulled on the chickens' legs, causing them to flap their wings and squawk. Amid the commotion created by the chickens, she bowed her head and hurried past the man.

Tubman owned one elegant silk dress. Wearing that dress allowed her to walk about a town with grace and dignity, casting the notion that she was a well-to-do free black woman. Another one of her costumes featured a sun bonnet with a wide brim. With the oversized bonnet perched on her head, she moved about with her face down, unnoticed by others.

Some reports said that Harriet Tubman could change her facial features at will. She was in her thirties when she performed most of her work liberating slaves. But if she wished she could alter her face and her character to that of a giggling young girl. Her favorite disguise was as an old woman who had lost her memory and appeared to be dim-witted. Associates claimed she somehow ordered her facial muscles to assume the wrinkles and creases of an aged person. One friend said that "she seems to have command over her face, and can banish all expression from her features, and look so stupid that nobody would suspect her of knowing enough to be dangerous."[13]

The approach to a farm containing slaves she intended to liberate was always a tricky matter. She usually tried to make her break for freedom with others on a Saturday night. If the slaves fled on Saturday night, the masters could not post a "wanted" notice in the newspapers until Monday morning. She always stayed a safe distance away from a farm. She gave a trusted friend word for the people to come out and meet

Tubman had many clever tricks she used to fool slave catchers and to conceal her identity. These traits helped her bring many slaves to freedom. This photo of Tubman (at far left) was taken around 1900 with other former slaves she had helped escape.

her. When possible, Tubman liked to join up with her escapees in a cemetery. There, the party could pray, sing songs over a grave, and pose as mourners.

If she had money, she took her band northward on a train. But trains posed problems. A passenger car offered no avenue of escape if a slave catcher or a sheriff decided to board and question suspected runaways. Most slaves could not read or write. To cast suspicions away from her, Tubman sometimes sat on a train seat pretending to read a newspaper. This act fooled slave catchers. Surely an illiterate runaway would have nothing to do with a newspaper. One time at a station in Maryland, she believed slave catchers were lurking nearby. So she bought tickets on a train heading *south*. No runaway would ride a southward-bound train, and the slave catchers looked elsewhere.

At times, Harriet Tubman obtained forged papers for herself and the people she was conducting. The papers were made to look like government documents certifying she and her companions were free blacks. Little is known about the people who did the forging. Such forgers probably had connections to the Underground Railroad. Though she could not read or write, Tubman was an excellent judge on the quality of forged documents. She had to pay the forgers. She would only pay those who did the best job.

In one mission, she liberated a young girl known only as Tillie. She and Tillie had forged papers and sufficient money. They hoped to buy tickets and board a northward-bound boat in the Chesapeake Bay. However, the ticket clerk suspected their papers were counterfeit and told them to step to the side while he issued tickets to other customers. The two sat on a bench. While waiting, Tillie grew so terrified she almost panicked. Tubman prayed. Over and over she murmured under her breath, "Oh Lord! You've been with me in six troubles, don't desert me in the seventh!"[14] (This was probably her seventh rescue mission.) The prayer must have been heard. The clerk changed his mind and allowed Tubman and Tillie to board the boat.

A Fearless Leader

Tubman had to assert firm leadership over bands of runaways. She allowed no whimpering or complaining when the journey got difficult. Also, once a person joined Harriet Tubman on the road to freedom, there was no turning back. One dark night, she led four fugitives through the Maryland woods. She was in an area of the state where she had never been before. The party came across an unexpected river. They walked the banks searching for a bridge or a boat. Unable to find anything, Tubman ordered her followers to wade the river on foot. No one knew the depth of the waters and the night was pitch dark. Two men refused to venture into the river. Without uttering a word, Harriet Tubman splashed into the river and trudged across. The two men, shamed by a tiny woman showing more courage than they did, followed her.

On another rescue mission, Tubman hid a band of runaways in a dismal swamp.[15] For a day and a night, the people huddled together in the wet grasses without

Slaves escaping to the North through southern swamps. Sometimes Tubman used swamps for concealment during her rescue missions.

food or warmth. One man grew discouraged and announced he was going back to his old master even if he had to face the whip. Tubman knew that the man could be tortured into informing on the others. Tubman frequently carried a pistol with her on her ventures to the South. She pointed the pistol at the man's head and said, resolutely, "Move or die."[16] The man resumed his walk to freedom.

Often Tubman was out of touch with her friends in the Underground Railroad for weeks and months at a time. Always her friends worried she had been captured. In 1857, Thomas Garrett wrote to William Still: "I have been very anxious for some time past, to hear what has become of Harriet Tubman. . . . It would be a sorrowful fact, if such a hero as she, should be lost from the Underground Rail Road."[17]

She was not lost. She was, instead, continuing her rescues, avoiding capture, and working her miracles. As one friend put it, "She could elude patrols and pursuers with as much ease and unconcern as an eagle would soar through the heavens."[18]

> **She pointed the pistol at the man's head and said, resolutely, "Move or die."**

Joe and Harriet: A Famous Flight to Freedom

Another of Tubman's rescue missions involved a slave who author Sarah Bradford called only Joe (known today as Joe Bailey). Bradford described Joe Bailey as

Taking Her Parents North

In 1857, Tubman returned to Maryland with the intention of transporting her parents to Canada. At this time, both her mother and father were free because Ben had bought his wife out of slavery several years earlier. However, Ben had allowed his house to be used by runaways. He also passed messages on from Tubman to the people she intended to liberate. Authorities were aware that Ben secretly aided runaway slaves (although they did not know he was helping his daughter). Ben's cabin was watched by slave catchers and sheriffs. Both parents were in their seventies and suffered several illnesses. They could not move fast. Despite these difficulties, Tubman escorted her mother and father all the way to Canada. Most of her brothers were living in Canada at the time, and they welcomed their parents with great joy.

being, "enormously tall and of splendid muscular development."[19] He was also a skilled timber cutter. Joe Bailey's owner hired him out to a fellow farmer who liked his work so well he bought him for the huge sum of two thousand dollars. When the new master arrived to pick up his "property," he whipped Bailey. This beating took place despite the fact that Bailey was an outstanding field hand and he rather timidly accepted his role as a slave. The master explained, "I always begin by giving [new slaves] a good licking."[20]

Joe Bailey was friends with Old Ben, Harriet Tubman's father. After suffering through the whipping, he made his way to Ben's cabin and said, "[Next] time *Moses* comes, let me know."[21]

In November 1856, Tubman led a party of four north toward freedom. Included in the party were Joe Bailey and his brother, Bill. The trip, which might have been Tubman's eighth, proved difficult from the start. Joe Bailey's owner discovered he was missing early and offered a huge reward of fifteen hundred dollars for his capture.[22] Dozens of slave catchers roamed the vicinity dreaming of arresting Joe, the high-priced fugitive.

As was customary, the group made its way northward mostly at night. This was no problem for Tubman who said that she followed, "the stars, and [could] find her way by natural signs as well as any hunter."[23] But the roads teemed with slave catchers. Because they were so eager to collect Joe's reward, they even ventured out in the bitter winter evenings.

Finally, the party reached Wilmington, Delaware, where they hoped to find lodging with Thomas Garrett.

However, Bailey's owner had arrived in Wilmington three days earlier. He put posters on buildings describing Bailey and announced his generous reward. Blacks, sympathetic to Tubman and the Underground Railroad, discreetly followed the owner while he pasted up the posters. When no one was watching, the blacks tore down the notices. But they could not remove all of the signs. Tubman determined it was too dangerous to take her band through the streets of Wilmington to reach the home of Thomas Garrett. The runaways had to stay in friendly African-American households on the outskirts of town.

Word got to Thomas Garrett that Tubman and her followers were hiding nearby. Garrett, always a clever Underground Railroad worker, sent a group of black bricklayers to pick up Harriet Tubman and her group. The bricklayers piled their bricks on a horse-drawn wagon in such a way as to create a hiding place for the escapees. Once they were hidden, the bricklayers drove toward the Market Street Bridge, which spanned the Christiana River. The bridge was in the most heavily patrolled part of town. Guards and policemen packed the streets near the bridge. The men drove along singing songs as if they were going to work. The songs distracted the guards. The wagon, loaded with its hidden cargo, crossed the bridge and left the town of Wilmington, Delaware.

Tubman and her group reached New York City. It is likely they rode a train at least part of the way. They still were a long way from safety. In New York's antislavery office, they were greeted by an abolitionist named

Oliver Johnson. It was there that Joe Bailey learned the full gravity of his high reward. Johnson showed him a reward poster and commented that, "the description [on the poster] is so close [to you] that no one could mistake it."[24]

The realization that he was such a hunted man almost defeated Bailey. Tubman intended to take the group to Canada, but Bailey still despaired. He believed he would never reach Canada with a small army of slave catchers after him. Throughout the long trek north, the fugitives had bolstered each other's spirits by singing hymns together. Bailey's was the strongest and sweetest voice of them all. But after New York he fell silent. Tubman said, "From that time, Joe . . . talked no more; he sang no more; he sat with his head on his hand, and nobody could 'rouse him."[25]

Tubman would not let Bailey's depression alter her course. She encouraged him to keep his hopes high, and she sang to him. Bailey continued to despair. The fugitives completed the last portion of their journey by train. Bailey sat silent all the way. The train crossed the bridge over the Niagara River and entered the free land of Canada. There it stopped at a station. In the distance the great Niagara Falls roared. Tubman said, "Joe . . . You're a free man."[26]

Finally, Joe Bailey understood. He was free for the first time in his life. Suddenly, the spirit of freedom charged his heart and filled his soul with joy. Bailey got off the car, stood on the station platform, and burst into song:

A painting of Harriet Tubman as she escorts escaped slaves into Canada. She led a group, including Joe Bailey, to Canada, despite the many slave catchers trying to find her party.

Glory to God and Jesus too,
One more soul got safe;
Oh, go and carry the news,
One more soul got safe.[27]

Bailey's singing was so powerful that he quickly attracted an audience. Harriet Tubman said, "The white ladies and gentlemen gathered round him till I couldn't see Joe for the crowd, only I heard his voice singing, 'Glory to God and Jesus too,' louder than ever."[28]

Chapter 6

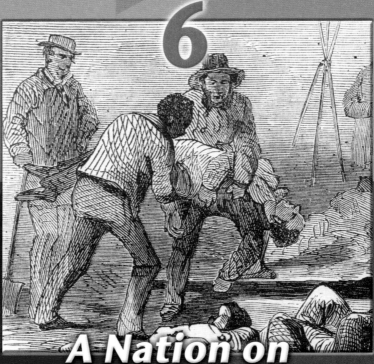

A Nation on the Brink of War

In May 1856, Charles Sumner, a senator from Massachusetts, took the floor of the U.S. Senate. Sumner made a speech denouncing slavery and condemning all those who practice or support the institution. Two days later, Preston Brooks, a congressman from South Carolina, confronted Sumner. The two argued loudly. Brooks raised the thick walking stick he carried and smashed it into Sumner's head. Again and again Brooks struck until the senator slumped to the floor. Brooks continued

Congressman Preston Brooks attacks Senator Charles Sumner on the Senate chamber floor in May 1856. The violent encounter exemplified the harsh division over the issue of slavery.

hitting the now unconscious Sumner until his walking stick broke.

This vicious beating within the U.S. Capitol Building was widely reported in newspapers, and shocked the country. Yet no one was surprised at the reason behind the violent confrontation—slavery. Throughout the 1850s, passionate arguments raged between proslavery and antislavery Americans. As the decade progressed, so did the intensity of the clashes. The country edged to the brink of civil war. Slavery was the spark igniting the coming conflict. Reaction to the Sumner and Brooks fight illustrated the nation's great divide. Antislavery Americans in the North demanded Brooks be arrested for his assault on Sumner. Proslavery people in the South sent Brooks dozens of new walking sticks to replace the one he broke while beating his enemy.

A Star Among the Abolitionists

Abolitionist societies flourished in the northern United States during the 1850s. The various groups met, sang songs, listened to speakers, published newspapers, and signed petitions demanding their government abolish slavery. Their meetings were lively. The groups broke certain unwritten "rules" of the time. Women were allowed to speak, even to mostly male audiences. This came at a time when women were expected to stay at home and tend to cooking and house-cleaning chores. Abolitionist organizations were early advocates of women's rights.

Another common practice at abolitionist meetings was having African Americans address white audiences. This too ran contrary to customs. Free blacks in both the North and the South lived in rigidly segregated societies in the 1850s. Many white Americans believed that blacks were an inferior race. Therefore, African Americans were deemed unworthy of lecturing to whites. But in abolitionist circles, blacks were allowed to speak. Most of the black speakers had been slaves. The stories they told were painfully true.

Frederick Douglass was a popular speaker in antislavery meetinghouses. A splendid orator, Douglass held audiences spellbound while he told of his own

The Book That Helped End Slavery

The greatest abolitionist book of the 1850s was written by a woman. Harriet Beecher Stowe (1811–1896) was born in Connecticut to a family of abolitionists. She worked as a teacher and as a writer. Stowe wrote poems, children's books, and adult novels. In 1852, she published her classic *Uncle Tom's Cabin*. It quickly became the country's best-selling novel. Some three hundred thousand copies were sold in the first year of its publication. The book gave a realistic and brutal portrayal of slave life. *Uncle Tom's Cabin* was praised by northern abolitionists, but it enraged southerners. In many southern states, just having the book in one's house could bring a jail sentence to the homeowner.

Shortly after the publication of *Uncle Tom's Cabin*, a staged version of the book appeared in theaters. It became a hit play. Harriet Tubman was living in Philadelphia when the play opened at a local theater. One of her friends urged her to see the play, but she declined. She said, "I [don't have] the heart to go and see the sufferings of my people played out on the stage. I've seen the *real thing*, and I don't want to see it on no stage or in no theater."[1]

Harriet Beecher Stowe published Uncle Tom's Cabin *in the 1850s and the book became the country's best-selling novel.*

escape from slavery. Another active speaker was Sojourner Truth (1797–1883). An ex-slave, Truth crusaded for the abolishment of slavery and for women's rights. Audiences were enthralled by Truth's deep voice, her quick wit, and by the Christian zeal she brought to her causes.

Harriet Tubman spoke at antislavery meetings in Pennsylvania, Massachusetts, and New York. Though a small woman, she had a commanding voice, which could be heard even in the back rows of a meeting hall. She told of her adventures leading runaways to freedom. Her stories, related in simple and direct language, never failed to capture the rapt attention of the audience.

Through Tubman's stories, the Underground Railroad rose to legendary heights in the minds and hearts of abolitionists. In the late 1850s, Tubman was one of its fund-raisers. When she gave a speech, people came. Because they were inspired by her words, they gave money to Underground Railroad organizations. Harriet Tubman both entertained and educated spectators. Her friend William Wells Brown wrote: "The most refined person would listen for hours while [Tubman] related the intensely interesting incidents of her life, told in the simplest manner, but always seasoned with good sense."[2]

Though Tubman was hailed by abolitionists, she was at the same time condemned as a criminal in her native state of Maryland. Shortly after she rescued a group of seven slaves in 1860, she spoke to an abolitionist group in Boston and drew wild cheers. The reaction of the Bostonians angered a Maryland man

Harriet Tubman spoke at many antislavery meetings, describing her missions leading escaped slaves to freedom. This is an antislavery meeting in Boston in 1851.

who wrote: "What could be more insulting after having lost [valuable] property by that deluded negress, than for a large congregation of whites and well educated people of Boston to endorse such an imposition on the Constitutional rights of the slave States."[3]

Slavery in the West

In the 1850s, the status of the new territories opening to settlement in the West became a subject of angry debate. The question loomed: Should slavery be allowed or forbidden in the West? In 1854, Congress passed the Kansas-Nebraska Act. It allowed settlers in the new territories of Kansas and Nebraska to determine if those regions were to be slave states or free states. The Kansas-Nebraska Act, though a compromise, angered both sides. It was followed by another controversial measure. In 1857, the Supreme Court issued the *Dred Scott* decision. The court said African Americans are not citizens of the United States, and therefore antislavery laws violate the constitution. The *Dred Scott* decision infuriated abolitionists.

Much of what the government did in the 1850s was designed to cool tempers. Leaders feared the country was slipping into a potentially violent division between the North and the South. For the most part, however, the government measures had the opposite effect. The court cases and acts of Congress only served to intensify the country's march to war.

Harriet Tubman and John Brown

Of all the nation's abolitionists, none was more fiery in his devotion to the cause than John Brown (1800–1859). Born in Connecticut, Brown worked his entire life to rid his nation of slavery. He was no secret member of the Underground Railroad. He let it be known loudly and clearly that his house was open to fugitives.

As was true with Harriet Tubman, Brown's antislavery zeal was based on religion. To Brown, slavery was an enormous sin. In the United States, it was a sin committed by the entire nation. As long as slavery existed in America, Brown reasoned, no American would be allowed to enter the kingdom of heaven. Some people, including many abolitionists, thought John Brown was a madman. Others felt he was a saint.

The operations of abolitionist groups were often slowed by too much planning and far too much talk. John Brown was a man of action. He viewed abolition as a holy war and regarded all proslavery Americans as his mortal enemy. He moved to Kansas to fight against the proslavery forces entering that state at a rapid pace. He wanted to keep Kansas from becoming a slave state. He also wanted to help some of his sons who had moved there. In May 1856, he and several of his sons murdered five proslavery men. The murders were deliberate, cold-blooded, and brutal. Brown and his followers hacked the men to death with swords.

Brown and Harriet Tubman met in New York in the spring of 1858. The meeting was arranged by several important abolitionists. At the time, Brown was wanted for the murders he committed in Kansas. Tubman was a runaway slave, and she risked her life because she helped other slaves find freedom. Both were fugitives from the law. Brown and Tubman bonded immediately and became friends.

In John Brown, Harriet found a spiritual brother. Brown, like herself, felt commanded by God to end the evil practice of slavery. If it took a war to rid the nation of slavery, so be it. Brown saw in Tubman a God-sent person, someone whose belief in the antislavery cause was as powerful as his own. He paid her the ultimate compliment by changing her gender. She was a soldier in the war against slavery. But to nineteenth-century male thinking, a woman could not be a soldier. So he

John Brown shared Harriet Tubman's passionate hatred of slavery. The two met in New York in the spring of 1858.

made her a man. In a letter to his son, Brown said, "*He Harriet* [the emphasis is his] is the most of a *man* naturally; that I *ever* met with."[4]

The Raid on Harpers Ferry

Brown told Tubman of a daring plan he had been contemplating. He intended to go to the South and seize an armory, a place where many weapons were stored. Once in charge of the armory, he would urge nearby slaves to break away and join him. All who did join him would be pronounced soldiers and given rifles. In this manner, Brown would create a country within a country. He chose a mountain spot to make his stand because a mountain position was easier to defend. That spot was Harpers Ferry, Virginia (now West Virginia).

Tubman agreed with the plan immediately. The seizure of an arsenal by escaped slaves would terrify the South. Such an act could trigger a war, which might finally end slavery. Brown asked Tubman to go to Canada and recruit soldiers among her followers there. The soldiers would be used in the initial attack on the arsenal. Again she agreed.

Many fellow abolitionists thought Brown's plan was too daring, too full of risks, and too violent. One of the doubters was Brown's old friend, Frederick Douglass. In a letter, Douglass said he feared Brown was "going into a perfect steel-trap, and that once in he would never get out alive."[5]

Ignoring all skeptics, Brown made his move. On October 16, 1859, Brown attacked and seized control of the arsenal at Harpers Ferry, Virginia. He had not given Tubman sufficient time to raise an army from the runaways in Canada. Brown had only nineteen follow- ers when he launched his venture.[6]

At first, the operation went well. Brown and his men reached Harpers Ferry before sunrise. They marched to the center of town and quickly occupied the armory. Only one watchman guarded the building. Once in con- trol, Brown announced, "I have possession now of the United States armory, and if the citizens interfere with me I must only burn the town and have blood."[7]

This region of Virginia held thousands of slaves and many antislavery whites. Brown expected these enemies of slavery to flock to Harpers Ferry, join him, and form an invincible army. This part of the plan failed miserably. No one came to swell his ranks. In just two days, an army unit commanded by Colonel Robert E. Lee, who was later the top-ranking Confederate general, marched into Harpers Ferry. A short but fierce battle broke out. During the fighting, more than a dozen raiders, townspeople, and soldiers were killed. John Brown was captured.

Many of John Brown's raiders were killed during the attack and battle at Harpers Ferry.

Tubman was in New York City when she was told about the failed raid at Harpers Ferry. The news upset her deeply. She had hoped John Brown's action would strike a powerful blow against slavery. After the failed attack, all seemed lost.

Brown was given a quick trial and sentenced to be hanged. On December 2, 1859, he was led out of a jail cell in Charles Town, Virginia (now West Virginia). His arms were tied behind his back at the elbows in what must have been a painful position. Still, he managed to give a guard a note he had written while in his jail cell. He was taken to a field a short distance away where he met his death on the gallows. The note he wrote in his cell spelled out his grim vision of the country's future: "I John Brown am now quite *certain* that the crimes of this *guilty, land: will* never be purged *away;* but with Blood."[8]

A Hard Push to War

On the surface, it appeared that John Brown's raid at Harpers Ferry was a colossal failure. Yet the raid hastened the final end of slavery. Brown hoped wealthy abolitionists would contribute to the militant movement he fostered in Virginia. A massive slave rebellion led by whites and supported by white money was every Southerners' nightmare. Such an uprising would turn the South into a slaughterhouse as slaves took revenge for hundreds of years of servitude and suffering. After the John Brown episode, Southern states formed strong militias. With Southern armies in place, war loomed ever nearer. Brown had predicted this turn of events in his last note.

Eighteen months after John Brown's execution, the American Civil War broke out. Brown was not forgotten during the brutal conflict. Northern troops marched into battle singing, to the tune of the "Battle Hymn of the Republic":

John Brown's body lies a-moldering in the grave,
John Brown's body lies a-moldering in the grave,
John Brown's body lies a-moldering in the grave,
But his soul goes marching on
Glory, glory, hallelujah!
Glory, glory, hallelujah!
Glory, glory, hallelujah!
His soul goes marching on![9]

The Amazing Rescue of Charles Nalle

In the spring of 1860, Harriet Tubman lived in Auburn, New York. She resided in a house sold to her by Senator William Seward, a prominent abolitionist. Seward admired Tubman's work on the Underground Railroad, and he gave her easy payment terms for the house. Tubman was still a runaway slave. In theory, she could be arrested and forced back into slavery. But Auburn was a strong antislavery community. Several houses in the town served as stations on the Underground Railroad. Slave catchers were afraid to venture there.

Harriet felt safe in Auburn, and she began moving several family members to her house.

Early in 1860, Tubman was invited to address an abolitionist meeting in Boston. She was still depressed over the death of her hero, John Brown. But she agreed to make the trip. On the way to Boston, she stopped in Troy, New York, to visit a cousin. That chance visit led to one of her most remarkable rescues.

In April of 1860, sheriffs in Troy, New York, arrested a fugitive slave, Charles Nalle. Two years earlier, Nalle had fled from a Culpepper County, Virginia, plantation. He took refuge in Troy where he worked as a driver on horse-drawn wagons. The authorities in Troy were alerted that Nalle was a runaway slave. Because of terms in the Fugitive Slave Law, police had no choice but to arrest him.

Troy had several active abolitionist groups. Nalle was held prisoner in a building downtown until a court could determine his fate. A crowd gathered outside the building, chanting and demanding Nalle's immediate release. The crowd was made up of both black and white people. Because he felt trouble was brewing, the judge posted guards and restricted those allowed inside to watch the proceedings. Anyone who the guards thought would spark disorder was denied entrance.

Most of Harriet Tubman's rescues came after careful planning. This time, she assisted Nalle almost by accident. She did know that a fugitive was being held in downtown Troy, and a trial was taking place. Almost innocently, Harriet came upon the scene outside the courtroom and decided to act. She reasoned the guards would not let her inside. But those guards were no match for Tubman, the master of disguise. She wrapped a cloak around her and picked up a basket full of food. Thus, she assumed her often-played role as an elderly woman. The guards let her in, perhaps thinking she was delivering lunch for the judge's staff.

Tubman stood in the back of the courtroom when the judge read his decision: Charles Nalle would be sent back to Virginia and returned to slavery. The courtroom exploded in shouts and curses cast by the abolitionists. Amid the commotion, Nalle dashed for the open window and climbed out on the ledge. The courtroom was on the second floor, and had he jumped, he certainly would have injured himself. Guards grabbed him and pulled him back inside. The crowd below witnessed this near leap and screamed at the court to free the man.

Harriet Tubman sprang into action. Still dressed as a frail old lady, she darted toward Nalle and grabbed his hand. Showing surprising strength, she wrenched Nalle out of the grasp of the guards and dragged him toward the staircase. Guards struck her with clubs. Yet she continued to pull Nalle out of the courtroom. Remarkably, she suffered no severe injuries. A witness said, "She was repeatably beaten over the head with policeman's clubs, but she never for a moment released her hold."[10]

Once outside, the antislavery crowd took Nalle to the riverfront. The intention was to put him on a boat and get him out of Troy. Nalle was now cut, bleeding, and dazed. At the riverfront he was recaptured by

One of the earliest views of Troy, New York, is shown in this photo taken around 1858 by James Irving. Tubman's rescue of Charles Nalle took place in Troy only a couple of years after this photo was taken.

police and returned to a building downtown. Harriet Tubman rallied the crowd. Led by her, the antislavery people of Troy broke into the building and reclaimed Nalle. A newspaper, the Troy *Times*, later reported: "Rescuers numbered many of our most respectable citizens—lawyers, editors, public men, and private individuals. The rank and file though were black, and African fury is entitled to claim the greatest share in the rescue."[11]

> **Once on the streets, she raced him to the riverfront with, "bullets whistling past."**

At the end of a wild and madcap day, Nalle secured his escape. Rumors said he made his way to Canada assisted by a mysterious, elderly black woman. In fact, he found a hiding place in the countryside near Troy. Nalle never returned to slavery. Tubman later claimed that at one point she placed Nalle over "my shoulder like a bag o' meal and took him away out of [that courtroom]." Once on the streets, she raced him to the riverfront with, "bullets whistling past."[12]

The Road to Fort Sumter

Harriet Tubman made her last rescue mission to the South in the late winter of 1860. She had intended to liberate her beloved sister, Rachel. When she arrived at her old home in Maryland, she discovered her sister had died. Though saddened by the loss, she took a party of seven slaves north to freedom. Despite her skill at disguise, it was difficult for her to move from place to

Abraham Lincoln was elected president in 1860. This election further pushed the United States toward a civil war.

place undetected because slave patrols were everywhere. Her last rescue, as was true of the earlier ones, was successful. She brought all her charges to freedom.

While Harriet Tubman concluded her work on the Underground Railroad, the nation moved steadily toward war. Two final steps made war inevitable. The first step was John Brown's 1859 raid at Harpers Ferry. That raid prompted Southerners to raise armies. The second step was the 1860 election of Abraham Lincoln as president.

Abraham Lincoln (1809–1865), a lawyer from Illinois, was not an abolitionist. He had no plans to free the slaves. Instead, he hoped that slavery would simply die a natural death. He was opposed to allowing slavery in the new states forming in the West. But Southerners widely believed Abraham Lincoln was an abolitionist who would immediately move to outlaw slavery. Fearing this event, South Carolina seceded (declared itself independent from the rest of the country) in December 1860. Before Lincoln took office on March 4, 1861, six more southern states had seceded from the American Union. The southern states formed the Confederate States of America, known as the Confederacy. The nation was now bitterly divided into two separate and hostile camps.

In late 1860, Harriet Tubman had a glorious dream, which she believed was a window to the future. At the time she was in New York, staying in the house of Henry Highland Garnet, a black abolitionist. Tubman joined Garnet for breakfast. She must have been in a marvelous mood. Her dream told her all of America's slaves were free. She practically sang out to Garnet, "My people are free. My people are free." Garnet said, "My grandchildren may see the day of emancipation of our people, but neither you nor I." Tubman insisted, "I tell you sir, you'll see it, and you'll see it soon."[13]

On April 12, 1861, just a few months after Tubman's dream, Confederate forces fired on the federal garrison of Fort Sumter in Charleston, South Carolina. The American Civil War began.

Chapter 7

War and Aftermath

The American Civil War lasted from 1861 to 1865. More than ten thousand battles were fought over land stretching from the Atlantic Coast west to New Mexico. Some three million men on both sides served in the military. About six hundred thousand—roughly 2 percent of the country's population—died in the fighting.[1]

The war pitted brother against brother and father against son. It shattered homes and disrupted families. Though it was bloody on an unimaginable scale, the war was the greatest turning point in American history. The terrible conflict destroyed slavery forever.

Tubman During the Early War Years

Harriet Tubman wanted to serve the Union in any way she could. But she was hampered by being a woman and by being African American. In 1861, there was no place for women as soldiers. Women could serve as volunteer nurses, and that is what Tubman concentrated on doing. Also, the military was a whites-only institution.

President Abraham Lincoln entered the Civil War with the intention of restoring the American Union, not freeing the slaves. The Union had been broken by the seceding southern states. Lincoln once said, "My paramount object in this struggle is to save the Union, and is not either to save or destroy slavery. If I could save the Union without freeing any slave I would do it, and if I could save it by freeing all slaves I would do it."[2]

In fact, early in the war, Lincoln viewed the immediate emancipation of slaves as a dangerous idea. Border states, such as Tubman's own Maryland, had not seceded. The president needed the border states to either stay neutral or to support the North. If Lincoln suddenly freed the slaves, those border states might lean toward the Confederate side.

Harriet Tubman disagreed with President Lincoln's approach to the war and to emancipation. She believed the Civil War was God's way of telling the nation to free its slaves. In early battles, the Union armies suffered

The Civil War lasted from 1861 to 1865 and thousands of people were killed on both sides during the bloody battles.

defeat after defeat. Tubman thought she knew why the North and President Lincoln were losing. She said, "God won't let Mister Lincoln beat the South till he does the right thing."[3] The right thing, in her mind, was to liberate all slaves.

> **"God won't let Mister Lincoln beat the South till he does the right thing."**

Harriet Tubman joined an all-women volunteer nursing group. Black women were allowed to give their services to such organizations. Many young soldiers suffered from dysentery and high fevers. Such non-combat sicknesses took more soldiers' lives than did battles and bullets. Tubman had treated diseases in her work as a conductor on the Underground Railroad. She made teas with special roots and herbs she found growing wild, and gave the tea to sick soldiers. She acquired the skill as an herbal doctor while assisting runaway slaves. Her treatments worked wonders. She helped many ill soldiers back to health.

In 1862, she sailed with Union forces to the Sea Islands off the shore of South Carolina. There, the Union army conducted operations deep in enemy territory. Tubman continued her work as a nurse. She also doubled as a cook and a laundress for soldiers. Some Northern soldiers recognized her as Moses, the famous conductor on the Underground Railroad. Her lectures at abolitionist meetings had given her a degree of fame. Said one observer, "[Union officers] never failed to tip their caps when meeting her."[4]

South Carolina slaves flocked to the islands held by the Union army. The slaves were afraid of the "Yankee" soldiers because their masters told them all Yankees had the horns and tails of devils. Still, many slaves believed this Northern army represented their best hopes for freedom. The slaves were put to work building fortifications for army camps.

General David Hunter, a Union officer in South Carolina, wanted to use the ex-slaves as more than laborers. Hunter was an abolitionist. He had known Harriet Tubman from abolitionist meetings in his home state of Massachusetts. Hunter dreamed of arming runaway slaves and turning them into soldiers. He also had a role for Harriet Tubman. Hunter hoped to use Tubman as a spy.

The Emancipation Proclamation

In Washington, President Abraham Lincoln slowly changed his views on emancipation. The war was going poorly for Lincoln and the North. If black men were willing to fight for the Union, why not give them a chance? As was true with other citizens, blacks needed a reason to fight. The president gave them a reason: freedom. Lincoln issued the famous Emancipation Proclamation, which became effective on January 1, 1863. The proclamation granted freedom to all slaves living in states that had seceded from the Union. It also said the North would begin enlisting African Americans into the army and navy.

General David Hunter wanted to use ex-slaves as soldiers. He also wanted to use Harriet Tubman as a spy for the Union Army.

The Emancipation Proclamation did not liberate slaves in the border states because most of them had not seceded. Nor did it free slaves in the Deep South because the Union army had no power in those regions.

However, the law enabled some one hundred thousand slaves to join the Union army, wear its uniform, and be paid by the federal government. The Emancipation Proclamation was an important first step toward ending slavery in the United States.

> **All present, including Tubman, sang "My Country 'Tis of Thee" and "John Brown's Body."**

The proclamation was greeted with great joy by African Americans. At Harriet Tubman's military post in the Sea Islands, soldiers were assembled and bands played. The soldiers stood at attention while the Emancipation Proclamation was read to them. All present, including Tubman, sang "My Country 'Tis of Thee" and "John Brown's Body."

A Soldier and Spy

Harriet Tubman was famous among the abolitionists in the North. But to the people in the Deep South she was hardly known at all. This, along with her knack for disguise and her ability to move about at night in country regions, made Tubman a perfect candidate to be a spy. General David Hunter wanted to hit the South in its financial heart—the cotton industry. He sent Harriet Tubman ahead to scout out the region's largest cotton plantations. Disguised as a half-mad elderly lady, she wandered over plantation property. Because she played her part so well, her spy missions were successful. She reported back to Hunter vital details such as the lay of the land and the size of the cotton plantations in the region.

General Hunter also instructed Tubman to spread the word that he sought slaves who wished to serve as soldiers. Many top army generals still opposed the idea of arming black men. Hunter dismissed his opponents. The slaves knew this territory and they knew the plantations. Hunter said, "We have wasted enough time. . . . I would advance south, proclaiming the negro free and arming him as I go. . . . [T]his is the only way in which this war is to be ended, and the sooner it is done the better."[5]

The Combahee River Raid

In 1863, Tubman joined an army unit called the 2nd South Carolina Colored Volunteers. It was one of the first army groups made up primarily of black soldiers. On the night of June 2, she and the other members of the unit boarded three Union gunboats, which steamed up the Combahee River in South Carolina. The unit of about 150 men was poised to raid several rich cotton plantations near the riverbank. In her role as a spy, Harriet had scouted this land. Now, as a soldier, she took the men into battle. The Combahee River Raid made history. It marked the first time an American

Soldiers from the 1st South Carolina United States Volunteers Infantry, another primarily African American regiment, in 1863. Tubman would join the 2nd South Carolina Colored Volunteers during the Combahee River raid.

woman—white or black—led American troops into combat operations.[6]

The raid was a stunning success. They burned tons of cotton and seized thousands of dollars in food and supplies. Months earlier, on scouting missions, Tubman had infiltrated these plantations. She told slave women to wait until they heard the sound of a boat whistle at night and then rush to the river. In the middle of the night came the loud, screaming shrill of a boat whistle. It set off an avalanche of slaves seeking freedom. "I never saw such a sight," said Harriet. "Here you'd see a woman with a [rice bucket] on her head. . . . One woman brought two pigs, a white one and a black one."[7]

About eight hundred slaves reached the riverbank.[8] Somehow, they all climbed on board the three gunboats and were carried to freedom. That one daring raid destroyed the productivity of the Combahee River plantations, and deprived the South of many thousands of dollars in revenues.

Free at Last

Gradually, the North's objections to using African Americans as soldiers faded. Toward the end of the war about 10 percent of the Union Army was made up of African-American men. Nearly forty thousand black troops died in the war years. Sixteen African Americans were awarded the Medal of Honor, the nation's highest decoration for bravery.[9]

By 1865, the Confederate Army had suffered a series of costly defeats. Union forces occupied large

"Glory"

The most famous all-black unit of the Civil War era was the 54th Massachusetts Infantry Regiment. The 54th was made up of black enlisted men commanded by white officers. In July 1863, the unit of some six hundred men charged the strong Confederate position of Fort Wagner in South Carolina. Almost half their number were killed or wounded. The 54th failed to capture the fort, but Union officers were impressed by the courage displayed by African-American troops. Their bravery in battle erased doubts held by many whites as to the fighting abilities of black soldiers. The 54th was stationed on the Sea Islands, and Harriet Tubman knew many of the men. Some reports say she cooked the last meal eaten by the comman- der, Colonel Robert Gould Shaw. Colonel Shaw was killed the next day during the attack. The 1989 movie *Glory* told the heroic story of the 54th Infantry and their bold assault on Fort Wagner.

The 54th Massachusetts Infantry Regiment charged Fort Wagner in July 1863.

parts of Confederate territory. On April 9, 1865, General Ulysses Grant of the Union army met with the Confederate general Robert E. Lee at Appomattox Courthouse in Virginia. The two agreed to surrender terms, ending the Civil War.

The issue of slavery had ruptured the American union. Finally, after more than two hundred years, the cruel system was abolished from the land. Slavery officially ended with the passage of the Thirteenth Amendment to the Constitution in December 1865.

Harriet Tubman learned that freedom did not mean equality. She never received payment from the government for her service in the Civil War. As a nurse, she was not entitled to pay because she served in an all-volunteer unit. But as a Union spy and as a leader in the Combahee River Raid, she certainly could have received the payment granted to a soldier. But she never received a penny for the deeds she performed.

Even Tubman's homecoming from the war was marred by a bitter experience. She rode in a passenger car on a train toward New York. In New Jersey, a conductor asked to see her ticket. She showed him the ticket, which had been issued to her by the army. It identified her as a soldier. The conductor could not believe that a soldiers' pass was given to a black woman. He ordered her to sit in the baggage car. She refused. The conductor tried to force her to move, but Tubman resisted. Four passengers helped the conductor drag her to the baggage compartment. In the struggle, she suffered a broken arm and other injuries.

Chapter 8

Reflecting on Harriet Tubman's Life

S peaking in 1867, abolitionist Gerrit Smith said, "I have known Mrs. Harriet Tubman for many years. Seldom, if ever, have I met with a person more philanthropic, more self-denying, and of more bravery."[1] The praises sung about Harriet Tubman, her life and her work, go on to this day. She is by every measure a genuine American hero.

The Later Years

After the war, Harriet Tubman returned to her house in Auburn, New York. There, she cared for her aging parents and took in black war veterans who needed help. One such veteran was Nelson Davis, who was more than twenty years her junior. Despite the age difference, the two fell in love. They were married in March 1869.

The couple never had children, but their marriage was certainly a happy one. Nelson Davis was particularly skilled as a builder. He expanded their house so they could take in more needy people. Davis and Tubman also ran a brick-making business. Working together, they grew fruit and vegetables in their garden and sold the produce at a city market. Much of what they earned went to support the destitute people the couple took in. A woman who lived nearby wrote: "All these years her doors have been open to the needy. . . . At no one time can I recall the little home to have sheltered less than six to eight [people] entirely dependent upon Harriet for their all."[2]

> **"All these years her doors have been open to the needy."**

Tubman was an active member of Auburn's African Methodist Episcopal Zion Church. Fellow church members said she had the sweetest voice in the church choir. Through the church, she worked to establish a home to care for elderly African-Americans. Raising funds for the home was a difficult undertaking. The Harriet Tubman Home for the Aged did not open until June 1908.

Long after the Civil War, she was called upon to give speeches about her Underground Railroad work. She peppered her speeches with songs. The audience loved her performances and donated money to her church and to her favorite causes.

Never did Tubman lose her sense of activism. She transferred her energies from abolition to women's rights. The demand for women's voting privileges (suffrage) grew in the late 1800s. Tubman joined the movement and soon worked beside famous suffrage advocates, such as Susan B. Anthony. It was a frustrating cause. The effort to secure women's suffrage endured many setbacks, as had the cause of abolition. Women did not win the right to vote in all elections

The Harriet Tubman Home for the Aged opened in June 1908.

The Harriet Tubman Home

Tubman's Auburn house and the home for the aged she established have been preserved and can be visited today. They sit on a twenty-six-acre parcel of land, which contains four buildings, two of which were used by Tubman and her family. In the 1920s, the houses on the site were abandoned, and the city planned to demolish them. However, the African Methodist Episcopal Zion Church bought the property and restored the buildings. The church owns the historic site today.

until 1920 with the ratification of the Nineteenth Amendment to the U.S. Constitution.

Poverty haunted Harriet Tubman throughout her life. Time after time, she applied to the government to be paid for her wartime service as a soldier and a spy. Always she was turned down. She earned a living working as a cleaning woman and a cook, and she took in boarders. The two books on her life, written by Sarah Bradford, made some money. She continued to give lectures. Requests for her speaking services dwindled as memories of the Underground Railroad faded.

Her troubles with sleeping sickness remained with her into old age. Rarely did she complain about her

This photo of Harriet Tubman was taken near the end of her life, probably at her home in Auburn, New York.

tendency to doze off and slip into a deep sleep. Friends thought the spells underscored her mysticism. When she fell into one of her sleeping periods, friends claimed, she visited a special world where angels and spirits dwelled.

In early 1913, Harriet Tubman believed she was about to die. She was, at the time, a resident at the home for the aged that she founded. Family and friends visited her often. On March 10, 1913, she was particularly sick and confined to bed. She told bedside visitors, "I go to prepare a place for you."[3] She then died peacefully.

The Harriet Tubman Legacy

Harriet Tubman's memory is kept alive today, particularly in the hearts and minds of the nation's young people. Scattered around the country are dozens of schools named in her honor: the Harriet Tubman Elementary School in College Park, Georgia; the Harriet Tubman Middle School in Portland, Oregon. The list of schools named after this brave woman goes on and on. Harriet Tubman is a genuine folk hero to children, and this is only fitting. She loved children when she was alive. She would be proud to know the story of her life still excites young readers today.

"I go to prepare a place for you."

Frederick Douglass, who always admired Harriet Tubman, pointed out that her heroic deeds on the Underground Railroad were performed freely. She risked her life liberating enslaved people, but received little or no money for her

Biographies of an American Hero

During Harriet Tubman's lifetime, Sarah Bradford published two biographies of her. They were the last major adult books written about her for decades to come. But starting in the 1950s, dozens of books for young readers telling the Tubman story appeared. They ranged from picture books for beginning readers to high-school biographies. Kids found the books to be interesting and full of adventures. As a result, American children knew more about Harriet Tubman than did their parents.

Recently two adult biographies of Tubman have been published. In 2003, author Kate Clifford Larson completed *Bound for the Promised Land: Harriet Tubman, Portrait of an American Hero.* In 2004, Catherine Clinton published *Harriet Tubman: The Road to Freedom.* Both are excellent books. Today, the gap is closed and parents can study the life of Tubman as avidly as did their children.

Landmarks of Harriet Tubman are all over the United States. This statue of Tubman leading a group of runaways was unveiled in Boston's South End neighborhood on June 20, 1999.

efforts. However, she did obtain the eternal gratitude of those she rescued. To a humble person such as Harriet Tubman, the simple "thank you, Moses" she heard from newly liberated slaves was payment enough. As Douglass put it, " . . . the most that you have done has been witnessed by a few trembling, scarred, and foot-sore bondmen and women, whom you have let out of the house of bondage, and whose heartfelt 'God bless you' has been your only reward."[4]

CHRONOLOGY

1793 —Eli Whitney invents the cotton gin, a simple device that makes processing raw cotton easier.

1808—By law, the importation of slaves from Africa and other countries ends; this law, plus the growing cotton industry, creates a greater demand for slaves in the Deep South.

1820 or 1822?—Harriet Tubman is born a slave in Dorchester County, Maryland; it is not known for certain if 1820 is her proper birth year because accurate records for babies born to slaves were rarely kept; 1820 is the year listed on her gravestone.

1827 —The young Araminta Ross (Harriet's name at birth) is "hired out" to work in a neighbor's house.

1831 —A slave, Nat Turner, leads a violent uprising in Virginia which kills fifty-nine whites; the Nat Turner Rebellion scares whites and prompts southern states to write new laws restricting the lives of all blacks, both slaves and free.

1844—Araminta Ross marries John Tubman and changes her first name to Harriet; she is now Harriet Tubman.

1845– 1849 —Great numbers of slaves are being sold from border states such as Maryland to cotton-producing states in the Deep South; rumors abound on Tubman's farm that she and others will be sold.

1849 — After one failed attempt, Tubman escapes slavery in Maryland and settles in Philadelphia.

1850 — The Fugitive Slave Act, which requires police to arrest escaped slaves anywhere in the country, is passed by Congress; in her first rescue mission, Tubman returns to Maryland and helps her niece and her family to escape.

1851 — Tubman rescues her brother Moses and several of his companions.

1852 — Harriet Beecher Stowe publishes her classic antislavery book *Uncle Tom's Cabin*.

1852–
1857 — Averaging about one rescue mission a year, Tubman liberates several groups of slaves; she also strengthens her ties with agents of the Underground Railroad who own houses along Maryland's and New England's "liberty lines."

1857 — Tubman takes her aging parents to Canada.

1858 — Tubman meets antislavery radical John Brown, who wants her to work with him and start a war against slavery.

1859 — John Brown's raid at Harpers Ferry fails and he is captured and hanged; the raid terrifies Southerners.

1860 — Tubman participates in an amazing rescue of Charles Nalle; Abraham Lincoln is elected president; Tubman conducts her last rescue mission.

1861 — Confederate forces fire on Fort Sumter on April 12; the Civil War begins.

1862—Tubman serves as a volunteer nurse tending to Union troops on the Sea Islands off South Carolina; Union officers recruit her to be a spy and to scout out large cotton plantations.

1863—Abraham Lincoln issues the Emancipation Proclamation, effective on January 1; Tubman becomes the first American woman to lead men into combat as she raids plantations along the Combahee River and frees some eight hundred slaves.

1865—The Civil War ends with the South's surrender; slavery is abolished with the passage of the Thirteenth Amendment to the Constitution.

1869—Tubman marries Nelson Davis in Auburn, New York; Sarah Bradford publishes her biography *Scenes in the Life of Harriet Tubman.*

1886—Sarah Bradford completes her second biography *Harriet Tubman: The Moses of Her People.*

1888—Nelson Davis, Tubman's second husband, dies.

1890—Tubman becomes active in the women's suffrage movement, which tries to bring voting privileges to the nation's women.

1896—Tubman buys land with the intent to open a home for elderly African Americans in Auburn, New York.

1913—Tubman dies on March 10.

CHAPTER NOTES

CHAPTER 1
An Incident in the Life of a Slave Girl

1. Kate Clifford Larson, *Bound for the Promised Land* (New York: Ballantine Books, 2004), p. 42.
2. Ibid., p. 44.

CHAPTER 2
Enduring Slavery

1. Geoffrey C. Ward, *The Civil War, An Illustrated History* (New York: Alfred A. Knopf, 1990), p. 9.
2. Catherine Clinton, *Harriet Tubman: The Road to Freedom* (New York: Little Brown, 2004), p. 16.
3. Peter Kolchin, *American Slavery 1619–1877* (New York: Hill and Wang, 2003), p. 94.
4. Kate Clifford Larson, *Bound for the Promised Land* (New York: Ballantine Books, 2004), p. 38.
5. Clinton, p. 5.
6. Kolchin, p. 156.
7. Sarah Bradford, *Harriet Tubman: The Moses of Her People*, originally published in 1886 (Mineola, N.Y.: Dover Publications, Inc., 2004), p. 14.
8. Clinton, p. 23.
9. Bradford, p. 10.
10. Clinton, p. 13.
11. Kolchin, p. 82.
12. Levi Coffin and William Still, *Fleeing for Freedom: Stories of the Underground Railroad* (Chicago: Ivan R. Dee, 2004), p. 55.
13. Larson, p. 78.
14. Bradford, p. 17.

CHAPTER 3
The North Star

1. *The Annals of America, vol. 8: 1850–1857 A House Dividing* (Chicago: Encyclopedia Britannica, Inc., 1976), p. 265.
2. Kate Clifford Larson, *Bound for the Promised Land* (New York: Ballantine Books, 2004), pp. 82–83.
3. Ibid., p. 85.
4. *The Annals of America, vol. 7: 1841–1849 Manifest Destiny*, p. 283.
5. Fergus M. Bordewich, *Bound for Canaan: The Underground Railroad and the War for the Soul of America* (New York: HarperCollins, 2005), p. 349.
6. Ibid.
7. David W. Blight, ed., *Passages to Freedom: The Underground Railroad in History and Memory* (Washington, D.C.: Smithsonian Books, 2004), p. 3.
8. Bordewich, p. 350.
9. Catherine Clinton, *Harriet Tubman: The Road to Freedom* (New York: Little Brown, 2004), p. 49.
10. Bordewich, p. 350.

CHAPTER 4
Riding the Underground Railroad to Glory

1. Sarah Bradford, *Harriet Tubman: The Moses of Her People*, originally published in 1886 (Mineola, N.Y.: Dover Publications, Inc., 2004), pp. 70–71.
2. Catherine Clinton, *Harriet Tubman: The Road to Freedom* (New York: Little Brown, 2004), p. 83.
3. David W. Blight, ed., *Passages to Freedom: The Underground Railroad in History and Memory* (Washington, D.C.: Smithsonian Books, 2004), p. 114.
4. Clinton, p. 83.
5. Ibid., p. 84.
6. Fergus M. Bordewich, *Bound for Canaan: The Underground Railroad and the War for the Soul of America* (New York: HarperCollins, 2005), p. 351.
7. Clinton, p. 84.
8. Kate Clifford Larson, *Bound for the Promised Land* (New York: Ballantine Books, 2004), p. 93.

9. Ibid., p. 86.
10. Bordewich, p. 353.
11. Ibid., p. 354.
12. Ibid.
13. Clinton, p. 91.
14. "The Life of Harriet Tubman," New York History Net, February 20, 2008, <http://www.nyhistory.com/harriet tubman/life.htm> (March 30, 2009).

CHAPTER 5

The Moses of Her People

1. Catherine Clinton, *Harriet Tubman: The Road to Freedom* (New York: Little Brown, 2004), p. 74.
2. Sarah Bradford, *Harriet Tubman: The Moses of Her People*, originally published in 1886 (Mineola, N.Y.: Dover Publications, Inc., 2004), p. 3.
3. Ibid., p. 19.
4. Kate Clifford Larson, *Bound for the Promised Land* (New York: Ballantine Books, 2004), p. 302.
5. Fergus M. Bordewich, *Bound for Canaan: The Underground Railroad and the War for the Soul of America* (New York: HarperCollins, 2005), p. 351.
6. Clinton, p. 216.
7. Ibid., p. 85.
8. Ibid.
9. Ibid.
10. Larson, p. 128.
11. Ibid., p. 137.
12. Ibid., 129.
13. Bordewich, p. 352.
14. Bradford, p. 33.
15. Clinton, pp. 90–91.
16. Bordewich, p. 353.
17. Clinton, p. 112.
18. Ibid., p. 91.
19. Bradford, p. 22.
20. Ibid., p. 23.
21. Ibid.
22. Larson, p. 134.
23. Ibid., p. 102.

24. Bradford, p. 26.
25. Ibid.
26. Ibid., p. 28.
27. Ibid.
28. Ibid., p. 29.

CHAPTER 6
A Nation on the Brink of War

1. Fergus M. Bordewich, *Bound for Canaan: The Underground Railroad and the War for the Soul of America* (New York: HarperCollins, 2005), p. 373.
2. Catherine Clinton, *Harriet Tubman: The Road to Freedom* (New York: Little Brown, 2004), p. 87.
3. David W. Blight, ed., *Passages to Freedom: The Underground Railroad in History and Memory* (Washington, D.C.: Smithsonian Books, 2004), p. 201.
4. Stephen B. Oates, *To Purge This Land With Blood: A Biography of John Brown*, second edition (Amherst, Mass.: University of Massachusetts Press, 1984) p. 242.
5. Ibid., p. 283.
6. Bordewich, p. 420.
7. Oates, p. 291.
8. Ibid., p. 351.
9. *The Annals of America, vol. 9: 1858–1865 The Crisis of the Union* (Chicago: Encyclopedia Britannica, Inc., 1976), p. 145
10. Blight, p. 196.
11. Ibid.
12. Kate Clifford Larson, *Bound for the Promised Land* (New York: Ballantine Books, 2004) p. 182.
13. Clinton, p. 136.

CHAPTER 7
War and Aftermath

1. "The Crossroads of Our Being," *The Civil War*, 2002, <www.pbs.org/civilwar/war/> (March 30, 2009).
2. Randall Bedwell, ed., *Brink of Destruction: A Quotable History of the Civil War* (Nashville, Tenn.: Cumberland House, 1999), p. 86.

3. Catherine Clinton, *Harriet Tubman: The Road to Freedom* (New York: Little Brown, 2004), p.162.
4. Ibid., p. 156.
5. Ibid., p. 154.
6. Fergus M. Bordewich, *Bound for Canaan: The Underground Railroad and the War for the Soul of America* (New York: HarperCollins, 2005), p. 431.
7. Sarah Bradford, *Harriet Tubman: The Moses of Her People*, originally published in 1886 (Mineola, N.Y.: Dover Publications, Inc., 2004), p. 53.
8. Ibid., pp. 52–53.
9. "Teaching With Documents: The Fight for Equal Rights— Black Soldiers in the Civil War," *The National Archives*, n.d., <http://www.archives.gov/education/lessons/blacks-civil-war/> (March 30, 2009).

CHAPTER 8
Reflecting on Harriet Tubman's Life

1. Sarah Bradford, *Harriet Tubman: The Moses of Her People*, originally published in 1886 (Mineola, N.Y.: Dover Publications, Inc., 2004), p. 73.
2. Catherine Clinton, *Harriet Tubman: The Road to Freedom* (New York: Little Brown, 2004), p. 203.
3. Clinton, p. 214.
4. Bradford, p. 70.

GLOSSARY

abolitionist—A person determined to end or abolish slavery.

activism—Profound interest in causes, such as women's liberation.

bondage—To be held to another person by law; a condition of slavery.

caulker—One who spreads tar on the seams of a boat to make it watertight.

deception—The practice of hiding one's true intent.

discreetly—To do something in secret.

elaborate—Complex or made up of many details.

enraptured—Enormous interest or devotion to something.

fugitive—A person wanted by the law.

hearsay—Something based on rumors, not established fact.

hypocrisy—Outwardly displaying feelings one does not really hold.

incursions—Invasions of enemy territory.

insurrection—An act of violent rebellion.

lore—Stories and legends growing about a popular person.

maladies—Sicknesses.

mystical—Something spiritual that escapes rational explanation.

ploy—A false action done with the purpose of disguising a true action.

prophetic—From the word prophet; someone gifted with being able to see the future.

refuge—A safe haven or safe resting place.

revenues—Income or money collected by a state in taxes.

ruse—A disguise, something done to hide one's true intentions.

sanctuaries—Places where one finds freedom from fear.

skeptics—Those who doubt.

strife—Tension or disorder.

underscored—To emphasize or stress something.

vendors—Sellers of goods.

zealous—To be passionately devoted to a cause or person.

FURTHER READING

Allen, Thomas B. *Harriet Tubman, Secret Agent: How Daring Slaves and Free Blacks Spied for the Union During the Civil War.* Washington, D.C.: National Geographic Children's Press, 2008.

Burgan, Michael. *The Underground Railroad.* New York: Chelsea House Publishers, 2006.

Fradin, Dennis Brindell. *Bound for the North Star: True Stories of Fugitive Slaves.* New York: Clarion Books, 2000.

Landau, Elaine. *Fleeing to Freedom on the Underground Railroad: The Courageous Slaves, Agents, and Conductors.* Minneapolis, Minn.: Twenty-First Century Books, 2006.

Malaspina, Ann. *Harriet Tubman.* New York: Chelsea House Publishers, 2009.

Martin, Michael. *Harriet Tubman and the Underground Railroad.* Mankato, Minn.: Capstone Press, 2005.

Skelton, Renee. *Harriet Tubman, A Woman of Courage.* New York: HarperCollins, 2005.

INTERNET ADDRESSES

Harriet Tubman.com
   <http://www.harriettubman.com/
   index.html>

Harriet Tubman Special Resource Study—
National Park Service
   <http://www.harriettubmanstudy.org/
   index.htm>

New York History Net—The Harriet Tubman Home
   <www.nyhistory.com/harriettubman/>

INDEX

HARRIET TUBMAN